# SHAKESPEARE'S PHILOSOPHICAL PATTERNS

WALTER CLYDE CURRY

# SHAKESPEARE'S
## Philosophical Patterns

GLOUCESTER, MASS.
## PETER SMITH
1968

This book I affectionately dedicate to

*My Former Students*

who visited in companionship with me
Shakespeare's cloud-capped towers, gorgeous palaces,
solemn temples—
and who wept with me at the death of old Kings.

# PREFACE

An expression of my appreciation is due to the editors of the North Carolina *Studies in Philology,* the *Journal of English and Germanic Philology,* and *Archiv für das Studium der neueren Sprachen* for their very courteous leave to reprint here, with some revision and corrections, the subject-matter of, respectively, Chapters II–III, IV, and VI. I am also greatly indebted to the kindness of the following publishers: namely, to the Macmillan Company for the privilege of quoting and basing arguments upon W. Windelband's *A History of Philosophy* (trans. J. H. Tufts), A. C. Bradley's *Shakespearean Tragedy,* and J. Lewis McIntyre's *Giordano Bruno;* to Messers Longmans, Green and Company for permission to use as herein indicated Maurice De Wulf's *History of Mediaeval Philosophy* (trans. E. C. Messenger), Eduard Zeller's *The Stoics, Epicureans and Sceptics* (trans. O. J. Reichel), and William Ralph Inge's *The Philosophy of Plotinus;* to Messers Henry Holt and Company for liberty granted to reproduce Pico della Mirandola's *Oration on the Dignity of Man* and a Letter to Ermolao Barbaro, from John Addington Symond's *Renaissance in Italy;* and to Messers Burns, Oates & Washbourne for the right to quote

v

and base arguments upon St. Thomas Aquinas's *Summa Theologica* as it appears in the authoritative translation prepared by the Fathers of the English Dominican Province. Without the gracious coöperation of these and other publishers, editors, and scholars, the appearance of this book must have been measurably delayed.

I take especial pleasure in acknowledging the invaluable criticism of the contents and organization of this work offered me by Professors John Crowe Ransom of Vanderbilt University and Robert Penn Warren of the Louisiana State University.

WALTER CLYDE CURRY

Vanderbilt University,
February 5, 1937.

# PREFACE TO THE SECOND EDITION

FOR MOST of my remembered life I have been profoundly attracted to the wisdom of Shakespeare. During my forty years of teaching at Vanderbilt University I observed with satisfaction how successive generations of my students were also inevitably drawn to the art of the great dramatist and had their hearts moved by his immeasurable sagacity. Members of these descendant classes have taught me much about human nature and have shown me how faithfully the receptive mind can reflect the more than brittle glory of the poet's imagination. The essays presented in this volume were originally conceived largely under the stimulus of student reaction. Since initial publication in 1937, the work has long been out of print. There have been recurrent requests for unavailable copies. I feel a particular joy, therefore, that the Louisiana State University Press has elected to issue a second edition.

Here are rosemary and rue, herbs of grace, for all those who reviewed my book after its first appearance. Some reviewers were most gracious in their general approval of the contents. Others seemed to feel that my purpose as indicated by the title was not fully realized. And others were definitely discontented with certain of my interpretations of the dramatic text together with my conclusions based upon them. But one reviewer did me an especial service: he pointed out that the volume as it stood was in great need of an index. I agree. So here is the Index. In the preparation of this latter item, I take singular pleasure in acknowledging the invaluable aid of Josephine Curry Raney, whose analytical insight is largely responsible for the balanced detail and excellence of scholarship attained.

I gratefully acknowledge indebtedness to Professor Hardin Craig, distinguished editor of Shakespeare's works, for his encouragement to me in my studies in Renaissance drama.

To Miss Jim P. Matthews, Order Librarian of the Joint University Libraries of Nashville, I pay tribute for her enthusiastic bibliographical skill which has so often befriended me.

How shall I thank my former student, Mr. Alfred Dandridge Sharp, whose long loyalty since his college days has brought him back on yearly pilgrimages to share *The Tempest* with me? The light of his spirit's ardor has been no brief candle in my memories as a teacher.

W.C.C.

*Vanderbilt University*
*April 18, 1959*

# INTRODUCTION

THIS essay is designed, in general, to indicate how Shakespeare came to participate in the philosophical traditions of his time and to illustrate his employment of inherited concepts as philosophical patterns of his dramas. It defines a philosophical pattern as any unified system of philosophy, involving definite relationships between man and an external world of given texture, which the dramatists may allow to serve as active, formative principle of his work.* Specifically, it attempts to show that the integrating principle of *Macbeth* is to be identified with a body of patrimonial doctrines transmitted to the Renaissance from the scholastic philosophers. Fundamentally, therefore, *Macbeth* is mediaeval and Christian. On the contrary, *The Tempest* is found to be formalized by traditional Neo-Platonic conceptions and may be considered, therefore, as being essentially classical and pagan in spirit.

Even so simple a statement of design must inevitably suggest the usual questions regarding Shakespeare's relation to philosophy. Did he have a personal philosophy of life, and is it recoverable from a study of his plays? Is it possible to demonstrate the

* For further discussion of patterns, see Appendix A.

immediate sources of his philosophical expression?
May he be considered as teacher and prophet? Was
he primarily a man of the Renaissance and, therefore,
immune to mediaeval influences? Without wishing to
controvert any studied opinion on such matters, we
may postulate certain positive and negative assumptions upon which this essay is based:

(a) Shakespeare was no systematic philosopher.
In these two contrasted works he is revealed as a
dramatic artist, who was capable to profound thought
and feeling in philosophical terms. But he has left no
evidence to the effect that he was either able or inclined to formulate an original philosophical system.
Like other men of his time he must, however, have
been acutely sensitive to the materials of philosophical traditions inherited from the past. And, if he
sought truth in this direction at all, his concepts of
man and the world were probably fashioned out of
principles furnished him by earlier or contemporary
thinkers.

(b) Shakespeare was artist rather than teacher.
These terms are assumed to be mutually contradictory. In *Macbeth* and *The Tempest* there is ample
evidence of the completely objective dramatist, integrating his materials in accordance with principles
borrowed from two contrasted philosophical systems.
Here may also be found wide illustration of the assimilation of philosophical expressions to dramatic
characters. But the author's intimate 'philosophy of

life,' if he had one, does not seem to be recoverable by means of any analysis or synthesis of his plays. He was neither prophet nor teacher.

(c) In matters pertaining to philosophy Shakespeare cannot be called a scholar in the narrower, humanistic sense. His knowledge of foreign languages, we may suppose, was comparatively limited. His interest may have at times been directed to philosophical questions as such, but it does not appear in his dramas. We cannot assume, therefore, that he ever read independently or deeply in systematic philosophy. Consequently, any inquiry which demands the immediate sources of his philosophical expressions is likely to be abortive and indeed futile.

(d) He does seem, nevertheless, to have possessed a comfortable and accurate knowledge of the basic principles supporting the two systems in question. Scholastic doctrine, transmitted by tradition, still persisted in the Renaissance mind as a heritage more or less unconsciously absorbed. Neo-Platonic concepts, likewise transmitted by tradition, had also become by 1610 largely anonymous and communal. And Shakespeare, like other men of his age, came to share in these respective patrimonies by right of inheritance and assimilation. The present study, therefore, concerns itself with the reconstruction of philosophical traditions—now almost forgotten—and with the dramatist's use of them. In the process of such reconstruction, however, it cannot undertake to furnish newly discovered materials for a history of philosophy; it merely re-orders, with special reference to Shakespeare, the established facts and principles of philosophical history and emphasizes certain aspects of philosophical speculation which may be unimportant to the historian but vital in an interpretation of the artist.

(e) Shakespeare's artistic supremacy does not necessarily imply his intellectual superiority. We have no reason to suppose that, as pure thinker, his opinions and beliefs were at all in advance of his time. Since he was no sëer, he cannot possibly have prefigured the modern advance in philosophy, science, or religion. He was rather immersed in the physical, mental, and spiritual life of his age. And his age was eminently pseudo-scientific and superstitious. Now whether or not Shakespeare the man believed in contemporary superstitions cannot be determined by any analysis of his plays, but we may assume that he followed the soundest opinion of his time. For our purposes in this study, at any rate, his belief or disbelief is of no importance. The significant fact is, as we shall see, that the sixteenth century, untrammeled by the rigid laws of modern science, supplied ideal food for the artistic imagination; and Shakespeare the artist, seizing upon it, assimilated it to his artistic purposes.

(f) This essay, moreover, does not recognize 'Shakespearean tragedy' or romance, in the sense

that the philosophical patterns of a group of plays
may be reduced to a single expression. It acknowledges only Shakespeare's individual dramas, each
one of which is a unique world unto itself, governed
by its proper laws, peopled by its special characters,
and integrated by a philosophical pattern separate
and distinct from all others. Individuals existing in
such disparate environments may indeed reveal acquaintance with fragments torn from the same philosophical system, but these expressions have usually
been appropriated to the dramatic characters as such
and, unless they present a generally accepted point of
view of the time, can offer little indication of the
philosophical pattern. For our purposes, therefore,
it is useless to seek confirmation of any conclusions
regarding *Macbeth* and *The Tempest* by reference to
any other Shakespearean works.

Formulation of these assumptions suggests that a
drama, such as *Macbeth* or *The Tempest,* may be considered as both artistic phenomenon and historical
fact. That is to say, as art-work it may be immediately
possessed by the contemplative spirit of men in any
age and under any circumstances; as a stimulus to
aesthetic experience it is timeless, self-sufficient, and
free. But as historical fact it must inevitably bear
upon it, in both form and content, the stamp of historical associations which influenced its production
and from which it emerged. Criticism, we may say,
attempts to report faithfully upon the efficacy of an

artistic construction as a stimulus of aesthetic experience; historical interpretation, on the other hand, is concerned with orienting the historical fact in relation to the historical events—traditional or otherwise—which urged the dramatist to create it. But wherever these scattered events originally focussed upon the drama have been forgotten, it is evident that criticism cannot exercise its function properly and completely without relying upon the findings of historical interpretation. Now this essay attempts no criticism of any play or group of plays; it offers no complete estimate of Shakespeare's art in the field of either tragedy or romance. In the interest of ultimate criticism, however, it does concern itself with historical interpretation, offering necessarily both general and specific observations upon the complex stimuli which aided in the production of *Macbeth* and *The Tempest*.

*We have lived illustrious, and to all posterity shall live, in the company of philosophers, conclaves of sages.*

PICO DELLA MIRANDOLA

# Chapter I

# LEGEND AND TRADITION: SCHOLASTICISM

I

That first, humanistic period of the Italian Renaissance which Shakespeare knew deserves critical examination without reference to later developments in art, science, religion, and philosophy. The intellectual history of this period—ending, let us say, around 1605–10—has been written from many points of view; but primary emphasis is usually laid upon the fact that here may be discovered the germs of our modern age, astonishingly crammed with achievement in the realms of thought and action. In the sixteenth century man is supposed to have rediscovered the world and himself; fetters which, in the Middle Ages, confined the human spirit within narrow limits, were broken, and one may view with satisfaction 'the modern rebirth of the individual soul.' We are told that the old theological scholasticism gave place to the spirit of free rational enquiry; the despotic spirit of the mediaeval Church fell before the awakening consciousness of the Reformation; the anonymity of

3

the Middle Ages was exchanged for the vitality and vigor of great personalities; superstition faded before the scientific investigation of nature; treasures of classical antiquity were reclaimed and assimilated —and in this manner the great modern age was 'gloriously inaugurated.' Having abstracted from their mediaeval setting such personalities as Chaucer and Wycliffe, Petrarch, Boccaccio, and Dante—who represent the flowering of mediaeval tradition—and having salvaged them to serve as initiating forces of the rebirth, writers on the Renaissance find the Middle Ages a dreary waste, upon which the modern period in its inception turned its back and which it ignored more or less completely.

For your chronicler of advancing thought, such a procedure of expiscating and stressing those new elements of the sixteenth-century complex which later proved most dynamic in shaping modern civilization is altogether meet and right. He may indeed take note of earlier and still persistent traditions, but his primary interest seizes upon certain virile forces which, at that time, were in process of opposing, transforming, and revitalizing the old order and initiating a swifter progress. But for the student of artistic phenomena in this period, on the other hand, the problem involved is entirely different and far more complicated. He must fix steadily in mind this axiom: the seventeenth century and its successors could have exerted no possible influence upon sixteenth-century accomplishment. He is not warranted, therefore, in superimposing upon Shakespeare's age any mode of thought—philosophical, theological, scientific, moral, or otherwise—which may have become peculiar to himself by virtue of his modernity. As disinterested critic, however, he cannot help recognizing that the sixteenth century was its unmistakable self: its civilization, like that of every period, produced by the urge of all preceding ages, the contents of its consciousness representing a curious mélange of ideas, principles, traditions which it gathered from all countries and periods of history, assimilated, and reshaped by its astounding vitality to its own uses. Shakespeare's world, with its unusual awareness of past achievements and with its promise of future development, ended in 1616. The honest student of Shakespeare's work, therefore, must be willing to entertain without prejudice any and all conflicting traditions, inherited from the immediate or remote past, which made this age rich and tumultuous. He will ignore no stimuli, of whatever origin or complexion, which rendered the sixteenth century particularly gracious in its influence upon the dramatic artist. Since his main preoccupation is not with the historical development of thought but with the emergence and growth of an artist, he will not be ashamed to admit that within the matrix of Renaissance culture there was a powerful infusion of mediaeval vitalism.

5

II

For prejudice originated and ignorance, in part, has perpetuated to this day the tough legend that the Renaissance disowned its mediaeval heritage, especially in matters philosophical. As everybody knows, the humanists interested primarily in literary style and averse to deep philosophical speculation, reformers obstinately opposing an established discipline, and scientists limiting their observations to material things—these created for later generations the myth that 'outworn scholastic learning, the relic of mediaeval monastic schools, was cast aside.' Erasmus, for example, was permitted a small 'drink of Helicon'; and after that experience he considered himself justified in scorning the 'barbarous' language and 'perplexing subtleties' of the entangled Realists, Nominalists, Thomists, Albertists, Occamists, and Scotists of his time.[1] His very soul was irked by the claim of ignorant scholastics to universal knowledge and by the arrogance and contempt of theologians, irritably disputing about 'trifles.'[2] In a 'witty and elegant' style he fleered at the mediaeval *Summae* and *Summarum Summae* written by 'saintly teachers, irresistible teachers, most subtle teachers, seraphic teachers,' reserving some degree of respect for Thomas Aquinas, however, who published certain commentaries on Aristotle, quoted Cicero and other

6

poets, and made some remarks about creation and the Trinity.[3] So Erasmus, skeptic, classical scholar, prince of humanists, and deliberate imitator of Italian humanists,[4] flouted the great thinkers of the mediaeval Church; but he did not reject or successfully controvert their fundamental principles. As a matter of fact, says Albert Hyma, 'whether Erasmus knew the scholastic productions himself is doubtful. He was falling into the same error of which many enemies of classical scholarship were guilty, namely, of condemning things they had failed to examine properly.'[5]

Reformers, moreover, eagerly encouraged and supported the humanist attack upon contemporary scholasticism. Martin Luther, for instance, was brought up in the 'modern' school of nominalism.[6] But when, under the inspiration of Augustine's philosophy, his personal reformation was accomplished, he violently repudiated the fundamental principles of the nominalist school.[7] His condemnation of these 'hog-doctors' whom he knew was unfortunately extended to the great mediaeval scholastics, Thomas Aquinas, Bonaventura, and others, with whose works he was but slightly acquainted except through the commentaries of his teachers.[8] And, naturally, he developed the greatest aversion for Aristotle, the magister of scholastic philosophy. The *Physics* and *Metaphysics* of this 'dead heathen,' said he, should be altogether abolished from the universities, together with all the other works which profess to treat of nature, though nothing could be learned from them, either of natural or spiritual things. The *Ethics* was directly contrary to God's will and the Christian virtues; *Of the Soul* had hindered and almost suppressed the books of the living God.

My heart is grieved to see how many of the best Christians this accursed, proud, knavish heathen has fooled and led astray with his false words. God sent him to plague us for our sins.[9]

In other words, the vehement genius of the practical reformer was able to draw but little inspiration from the cool rationality of Aristotle's system or from the intellectualism of the best mediaeval thinkers.[10]

Likewise, Francis Bacon, the scientist, could not abide either the form or the content of scholastic philosophy. He observed that, in proportion as humanistic stylists almost deified Cicero and Demosthenes, 'then grew the learning of the schoolmen to be utterly despised as barbarous.'[11] He scorned the 'unprofitable subtilty,' the 'fruitless speculation,' and the 'monstrous altercations' of those scholastics who permitted sound knowledge to putrefy under their hands into 'vermicular questions, having certain quickness of life and spirit, but no strength of matter or excellence of quality.'[12] Here spoke the exponent of empiricism, for whom 'the human mind, if it acts upon matter, and contemplates the nature of

8

things, and the works of God, operates according to the stuff, and is limited thereby.' [13] It is easy to understand, therefore, how such a materialist should have adopted an attitude of disinterested, and apparently contemptuous, silence toward those profound ontological questions which engaged the scholastic mind; [14] all such speculations were 'subtilities and matters of no use,' and seemed to him an 'old man's idle talk.' [15] Here the substance of scholastic philosophy was brusquely waived, it is clear, merely because the scientific mind found it uncongenial.

In this manner sixteenth-century prejudice, ignorance, and indifference established firmly the legend that scholastic philosophy became at that time outworn. Succeeding centuries repeated the charge of its subjection to Aristotle and Catholic theology, jeered again at its barbarous language, ridiculed its subtleties, expressed contempt for its puerile speculations, 'dealing with such questions as that of matter and form, powers and faculties, essence and existence.' [16] So persistent and universal was the condemnation that apparently nobody, until the middle of the nineteenth century, seems to have conceived of actually re-examining the great body of mediaeval philosophy with the idea of determining and justly evaluating its fundamental principles.[17] But even so, in spite of advancing mediaeval studies, only recently has the surmise been expressed that the sixteenth-century rebirth was not accomplished without participation of philosophical concepts elaborated in the Middle Ages. Indeed in some quarters the old legend still flourishes. In 1911 Preserved Smith could write: 'Mediaeval thought had progressed little, if at all, beyond Aristotle.' [18] In 1924 W. H. Hudson was still echoing the humanists on 'the sterility of that mediaeval theological philosophy which we know as Scholasticism,' and asserting that 'it finally disappeared under the combined influences of the religious and scientific movements of the Renaissance.' [19]

One humanist, however, did not fail to recognize the essentials of scholastic philosophy and to entertain graciously the values of scholastic tradition. It was Pico della Mirandola who scorned the trivial questions raised by stylists of his time and sought the 'soul of truth' which, he believed, vitalizes the scholastic as well as other systems.[20] In a letter to Ermolao Barbaro, for example, he revealed his attitude strongly:

And that I meantime should have lost in the studies of Thomas Aquinas, John Scotus, Albertus Magnus, and Averrhoes the best years of my life—those long laborious vigils wherein I might perchance have made myself of some avail in polite scholarship! The thought occurred to me, by way of consolation, if some of them could come to life again, whether men so powerful in argument might not find sound pleas for their own cause; whether one among them, more eloquent than Paul, might not defend, in terms as free as possible from barbarism, their barbarous style, speaking perchance after this fashion: ''We have lived illustrious,

friend Ermolao, and to posterity shall live, not in the schools
of the grammarians and teaching places of young minds,
but in the company of the philosophers, conclaves of sages,
where the questions for debate are not concerning the mother
of Andromache or the sons of Niobe and such light trifles,
but of things human and divine; whereof we have been so
subtle, searching and eager that we may sometimes have
seemed to be too scrupulous and captious, if indeed it be
possible to be too curious or fastidious in seeking after truth.
Let him who accuses us of dullness, prove by experience
whether we barbarians have not the god of eloquence in our
hearts rather than on our lips; whether if the faculty of
ornamental speech be lacking, we have wanted wisdom; and
to trick out wisdom with ornaments may be more a crime
than to show it in uncultured rudeness.'' [21]

We shall see presently to what extent he levied upon
the wisdom of these same barbarians when he came to
formulate his Renaissance definition of the dignity of
man.

III

For the scholastic synthesis represented in its
golden age not merely a splendid body of doctrines,
but also a form of thinking and a way of life. Any
statement, therefore, regarding the 'disappearance
of scholastic philosophy before the combined attacks
of humanism and the reformation' must be hedged
about with limitations and qualifications; the truth
inhering in such a formula must be carefully defined.
Your historian of thought and culture will indeed

11

recognize that the scholastic movement reached its height in the thirteenth century and that its decline through the succeeding centuries was marked by a progressive intellectual sterility. He will record the gradual disintegration and dissipation, through the fifteenth and sixteenth centuries, of the doctrinal heritage transmitted from the thirteenth century: here Nominalists and Realists fought out their mutually destructive battles; Thomists, Scotists, Occamists, and others strangled creative thought with futile distinctions and fervid commentaries upon principles handed down by the masters. Scholasticism *as a movement* was moribund; and though it straggled along throughout the sixteenth century in conflict with newer and more virile forces, it had *as a way of life* lost its universal efficacy.[22] And against this effete Scholasticism of their own day the humanists and reformers arrayed themselves.

The clear-sighted historian, however, will not fail to emphasize the persistent vitality of scholastic *tradition,* as distinguished from the historical movement. For this was the age of warring traditions, when primitive theology and ancient philosophy were revived and engaged in conflict with the mediaeval without definite conclusion.[23] The schools were tottering, but under Jesuit leadership the Catholic Church established the essentials of its dogma upon the philosophical doctrines of Thomas Aquinas.[24] The Reformation might return to St. Augustine for

12

inspiration, but it could not escape the mysticism of the Middle Ages [25] or complete its structure without reference to first principles laid down by the scholastics. Moral philosophy was a curious hodge-podge of ancient learning and scholastic ethics.[26] As Windelband remarks: 'All beginnings of modern philosophy have in common an impulsive opposition against "Scholasticism," and at the same time a naïve lack of understanding for the common attitude of dependence upon some one of its traditions, which they nevertheless all occupy.' [27] And De Wulf observes that certain elements of the scholastic patrimony 're-flect the Western mind too faithfully for the seventeenth, eighteenth, and nineteenth centuries . . . to forget them altogether.' [28]

Here is an astonishing situation which provokes consideration: writers of the humanistic period, while making a great show of dependence upon classical and other ancient sources (see lines and reference), nevertheless employed extensively certain fundamental materials of the scholastic tradition, usually without acknowledgment. Whether this notorious failure to credit scholasticism with the values it furnished was deliberate, contemptuous, and fashionable, or merely due to unconscious assimilation and reproduction of a common heritage, cannot be immediately determined. But that modern criticism should also ignore the debt is indefensible. Then let us examine, for instance, with a mind unprejudiced

13

by Renaissance rhetoric or modern rhapsody, the contents of Pico's celebrated *Oration on the Dignity of Man:*

Then the Supreme Maker decreed that unto Man, on whom he could bestow nought singular, should belong in common whatever had been given to His other creatures. Therefore he took man, made in his own individual image, and having placed him in the center of the world, spake to him thus: 'Neither a fixed abode, nor a form in thine own likeness, nor any gift peculiar to thyself alone, have we given thee, O Adam, in order that what abode, what likeness, what gifts thou shalt choose, may be thine to have and to possess. The nature allotted to all other creatures, within laws appointed by ourselves, restrains them. Thou, restrained by no narrow bonds, according to thy own free will, in whose power I have placed thee, shalt define thy nature for thyself. I have set thee midmost the world, that thence thou mightest the more conveniently survey whatsoever is in the world. Nor have we made thee either heavenly or earthly, mortal or immortal, to the end that thou, being, as it were, thy own free maker and molder, shouldst fashion thyself in what form may like thee best. Thou shalt have power to decline unto the lower or brute creatures. Thou shalt have power to be reborn unto the higher, or divine, according to the sentence of thy intellect.' Thus to man, at his birth, the Father gave seeds of all variety and germs of every form of life.[29]

Now aside from a peculiar emotional exaltation—a wild surmise as of the discoverer—which informs this passage, the mediaeval mind would recognize here some of its most intimate, comforting, and universally accepted doctrines. The Christian God reappears as Supreme Maker of a perfectly familiar geocentric cosmos; the apotheosis of Man as a microcosm reaffirms the anthropocentric conception of scholasticism. Indeed 'it is a commonplace of the schools [30] that man is a little world, in which we may discern a body mingled of earthly elements, and ethereal breath, and the vegetable life of plants, and the senses of the lower animals, and reason, and the intelligence of angels, and a likeness to God.' [31] God's granting him the psychological liberty of free-choice 'according to the sentence of intellect' recalls the mediaeval controversy over the relative superiority of will or intellect and establishes Pico, the good Catholic, in the Thomist tradition. The mediaeval mind could heartily approve the central place here given to the Supreme Creator, this recognition given to the dignity of human intelligence, and the respect shown for personality, 'which is but the application to man of the pluralistic conception of the universe.' [32] But the scholastic mind, with its devotion to abstract ideas, its analytical temper, and moderation, would scarcely have sympathized with Pico's rapture and immoderate utterance, which pronounce his spirit thoroughly Renaissance.

Approximately a century later, when the turbid mixture of the humanistic period was in process of clarifying itself, writers of a philosophical disposition were still drawing their premises from the scholastic patrimony. In 1594, for example, Richard

15

Hooker published his *Of the Laws of Ecclesiastical Polity,* a defense of Anglicanism and freedom of thought against Puritan attack. But Book I of his work is devoted to a clear exposition of the first principles of Law and its universal application, which constitutes a restatement of the scholastic position. Here,[33] as in the scholastic formulation, is affirmed the Oneness of God and the heterogeneity of his universe, created not according to the necessity of his nature (Neo-Platonism) but by a fiat of will (206) subject to the laws of his Being (199).[34] The disposition in God's own knowledge and will of created things according to their natures is rightly called Providence (209);[35] the execution of providential design is Government (210). Since creation is ordered in conformity with certain exemplary draughts or patterns (exemplarism) subsisting in the bosom of the Highest (208), it follows that all things, so long as they keep those forms which give them being, are subject immediately to God the efficient cause (204).[36] But in government the type of Divine Wisdom, moving all things to their appointed end—'any kind of rule or Canon, whereby actions are framed'—bears the character of Law.[37] Now the Eternal Law is, according to Hooker, 'that order which God before all ages hath set down with himself, for himself to do all things by' (203), not merely, as some say, 'that which with himself he hath set down as expedient to be kept by all his creatures' (204).[38] But whether we call

16

Eternal Law the reason of order or the execution of order, all other laws—Nature's Law,[39] the Law of Reason, and Human Law [40]—are dependent from it and necessarily participate in it (204). All natural agents, for example, must observe the Law of Nature because through it they have imprinted upon them the Eternal Law, from which are derived their respective inclinations to their proper ends and acts (209). They are God's instruments. Moreover, the hierarchy of angels, subject to the higher law, must necessarily participate of Eternal Law (211–214).[41]

But among all earthly creatures, that rational creature, Man, is subject to the Eternal Law in the most excellent way possible: he is provided with the light of natural reason, the imprint of Eternal Reason, whereby he may know good from evil (221).[42] The precepts of the Law of Reason impel him naturally toward his proper end and act (227).[43] And since he is yet 'somewhat in possibility,' his 'appetite or desire' urges him to greater and greater perfections (214). Thus the law of potency and act [44] is seen to operate, not only in the unconscious striving of natural agents for the realization of their natures, but also in man's conscious aspiration for the knowledge of truth and conformity with God (215). And man's soul, at first a *tabula rasa*,[45] rises to a knowledge of both sensible and intelligible things through education and instruction in the light of natural reason (218–19).[46] He is endowed with the psychological liberty of free choice and the ability to control the end which he pursues, namely, goodness or the actuation of all his potentialities (220). Since goodness is perceived by the eye of the intellect and the light of the eye is reason, the two principal fountains of human action are Knowledge and Will; and the Will in process of tending toward the good or apparent good—it cannot desire evil as evil (222)—is termed free-choice (220).[47] In proportion, therefore, as intellect is led astray in its judgments by defective knowledge, the will follows the wrong direction and man falls into sin (224). He may also err when passions, reinforced by habit (223), so fascinate the will by their show of temporal felicity that it is led to prefer the lesser good to that ultimate good which reason might dictate (220–223).[48]—And so on. In this manner Hooker would establish the foundations of his argument upon principles which, though discovered at first by discourse, are nevertheless 'drawn from out the very bowels of heaven and earth' (229).

Students of mediaeval philosophy cannot fail to recognize that Richard Hooker has, in this case, levied heavily upon the scholastic formulation of basic principles. God here reappears as voluntary creator of his universe according to a providential plan involving exemplarism; he governs through the conception and execution of Eternal Law, from which all other laws depend, and by means of appointed ministers. Here the Aristotelian theory of potency

18

and act is invoked and applied to incorporeal realms, in order that the process of man's attainment of ultimate being may be rationalized. Man participates of Eternal Law through the Natural Law [49] according to the implanted *dictamen* of his rational nature; and all human actions are subject to the psychological determinism of the Thomist school. In fact, Hooker might well have drawn the essential features of his discourse upon law and its universal application directly from the closely reasoned system of Thomas Aquinas. On unimportant points he quotes from Homer, Mercurius Trismegistus, Anaxagoras, Plato, the Stoics, and Hippocrates; he mentions Dionysius, paraphrases from Boethius, and cites the Scriptures. But regarding scholastic sources of the substantial content of his exposition, he is, like many another writer of the sixteenth century, completely silent. Why?

IV

A concerted impulse in the sixteenth century to ignore the debt to scholastic tradition was perhaps both conscious and subliminal. Undoubtedly, as we have seen, it was fashionable for humanists, reformers, and others to sneer at contemporary scholasticism; and insults directed at its form and content were deliberately studied. Some elements of the opposition had never read for themselves the works contemned;

19

others, while revolting against contemporary teachings, had never investigated at first hand the mediaeval body of doctrines; others were frankly uninterested in certain types of questions raised by the schoolmen. Yet all seem to have been thoroughly acquainted with scholastic tradition and to have depended—with what Windelband has called 'a naïve lack of understanding'—upon some one of its principles. Here we face a perplexing phenomenon. Perhaps, as De Wulf suggests,[50] the scholastic synthesis reflected the Western mind too faithfully for its doctrinal patrimony to be forgotten—even in the Renaissance. It may be that, though the mediaeval system of philosophy as a rigid pattern of life had collapsed, that pattern 'remained in all men a fixed point of reference for their sensibilities.'[51] Or, more likely, the scholastic heritage survived in this period as the primary groundwork of traditional cognition. Here was a vital body of doctrines and ideas skillfully built into a complex intellectual system, which in the Middle Ages had served universally as the foundation of social institutions, political theories, and religious faith. It exerted such a unifying effect upon mediaeval life and activity that the attitudes which it created became, as it were, communal; its essential principles were axiomatic. Learned men and the masses alike shared, according to capacity, in the common fund of knowledge, were actuated by the same modes of thought, and came to *assume* the validity of the

20

scholastic *Weltanschauung*. For almost eleven centuries this knowledge, these modes of thought, this way of life had been in process of shaping the very character and conscience of Western peoples. Thus cognition became so traditional that in a sense it may be said to have been congenital.

How, then, should the humanistic period hope to escape the discipline of eleven mediaeval centuries? The sixteenth-century mind was perturbed and, except for its grasp of mediaeval validities, subject to the near-chaos produced by conflicting influences; it is distinguished for its eclecticism and propensity to synthesis rather than for originality of intellection. Antiquity furnished it with a plethora of newly discovered ideas, doctrines, theories, systems of thought and fragments of wisdom, strange traditions, alien legends—a foison of quaint and forgotten lore—which it devoured with uncritical gusto. It became a perfect type of the young *intellectuel,* making a brave show of sophistication, ruffling it in the magnificence of Greece and Rome—an exoteric, fumbling with the mysteries—and professing to have abjured the moral nature transmitted and fostered by plain but honest ascendants. But observe: in the midst of the confusion and elegant shouting of this period, the verities of scholastic tradition still remained established and unmoved; something like a derived Natural Law, the tradition still impressed its precepts upon the minds of men and served as fundamental

21

principles of human activity. That is to say, the scholastic deposit represented the stable point from which all excursions were made; it was the intimate standard by which values of the new learning were consciously or unconsciously measured. It was the foundation upon which were erected many outlandish super-structures—both pagan and Christian—but it was nevertheless still sound and ineradicable. It had become, in short, the primary groundwork of cognition.

Consequently, when principles of the scholastic patrimony moved upon the mind of a sixteenth-century writer, they must have come with something approaching the authority of innate ideas. If one, like Pico, wanted to energize in pagan manner over a mediaeval concept of man's dignity in the universe, nobody thought of demanding documentation for the concept; it was his by right of inheritance and assimilation. If a Hooker based his argument upon scholastic principles without giving specific credit, he was probably merely reasoning from the axiomatic to new conclusions. Edmund Spenser proposed to build the twelve books of his epic around the twelve moral virtues of 'Aristotle and the rest,' but no one need suspect abnormality or subterfuge if the number of virtues turned out to be not Aristotelian at all but Thomist.[52] Indeed, moral philosophy of the Renaissance in general constituted at bottom a restatement and elaboration of mediaeval conceptions; [53] and the

22

faculty psychology of the time, involving the science of human passions, was 'the psychology of Aristotle and Bacon and of all the thinkers who lived between them.' [54] Students of the humanistic period, therefore, must learn to think in terms of generally accepted traditions rather than always of specific and direct lines of reference.

Now Shakespeare was a product of this age. It is not surprising, therefore, to discover that he also came to share in the scholastic patrimony. If he alone of all men had escaped such participation, that fact would provide cause for huge astonishment. He was, as De Wulf has observed, acquainted not only with the 'current coin' of scholastic terms but also with the traditional doctrines: Hamlet's 'table of my memory' upon which are written 'all forms, all pressures past that youth and observation copied there' reproduces the *tabula rasa* and the *formae et species impressae* of the schoolmen; his 'quiddities' in the sense of 'realities,' his 'god-like reason' which differentiates man from the beasts, his 'Sense sure you have, else could you not have motion' recalling the doctrine that movement presupposes sense-perception [55]—all indicate dependence upon scholastic principles, for which no immediate sources are available or needed. Such doctrines, as we have seen, were the common property of philosophers; and the poet absorbed them no doubt by the process of traditional cognition and assimilated them to the stuff of

23

poetic drama. His scholarship was probably too un-
disciplined to warrant the assumption that he examined for himself the works of scholastic philosophers,
but he nevertheless commanded, by processes indicated, the broad concepts of scholastic metaphysics:
that Christian cosmology postulated by his age and
the ontology which involved man as rational being
in definite relationships with a pluralistic universe.

And it is evident that these concepts, however mas-
tered, were allowed to integrate the contents of his
*Macbeth* and to determine the progress of both internal and external action. But whether he consciously or unconsciously adapted scholastic metaphysics to the uses of philosophical pattern of his
tragedy, cannot be ascertained precisely. Since, however, he was a creative artist and the knowledge concerned was traditional, we may presume that the
process of its employment was parcel intuitive; but it
also represented, in largest measure, the collaboration
of active and deliberative consciousness. At any rate,
when an investigator comes to observe the operations
of scholastic metaphysics as philosophical pattern
of *Macbeth,* he must remember that the energy directing those operations was not primarily philosophical
but artistic; and he must recognize that the principles
utilized, being traditionally transmitted, are not ref-
erable to immediate origins. Before he can understand the drama, therefore, he must reconstruct and
synthesize the whole scholastic background, in so far

as it may be seen to affect *Macbeth*. That is to say, his reorganization of background for the modern mind —in which the scholastic heritage has dwindled almost to nothing—must include detailed analyses of various scholastic systems, with which Shakespeare was totally unacquainted, as well as a synthesis of those principles which constituted the patrimony that Shakespeare possessed. Thus his primary objective will not be the orientation of the dramatist with reference to the complexities of mediaeval philosophy; but he will mainly concern himself with clarifying for the modern mind, with every pertinent detail of background available, those doctrines of the scholastic tradition which the artist has used in the externalization of his work of art. These purposes and these methods will be found to obtain in our discussion of *Macbeth*.

*Omnium quippe rerum quae cor-
poraliter visibiliterque nascuntur,
occulta quaedam semina in istis
corporeis mundi hujus elementis
latent.*

ST. AUGUSTINE

## Chapter II

## TUMBLING NATURE'S GERMENS

### I

A PHILOSOPHICAL pattern, we may recall, is a unified system of philosophical principles which the artist allows to integrate the contents of his drama. It involves a set of relationships linking human beings of specified nature to the spiritual and natural forces of the external world explicitly defined. In our discussion of the philosophical pattern of Shakespeare's *Macbeth*, therefore, it becomes necessary to consider in detail the two terms of such relationships: namely, Macbeth the man and the realities which surround him. This is not an easy procedure because Macbeth's character is itself infinitely complex and because Renaissance philosophy is syncretic in character.

But—observing first the texture of the external world to which Macbeth is related—we must recognize that nature-philosophy of the humanistic period centers generally about definite concepts of the 'virtues of things.' It is evident that most philosophers of this time who speculate upon the structure and movements of the material world and scientists who experiment

29

with its elements conceive of a formative principle with active and passive aspects which constitutes the essence of individuals in a substantial universe. Systems of cosmology may be traditionally pluralistic or monistic, creative or emanative, hylozoic or hylomorphic, but for the Renaissance mind there may be found somewhere near the core of creative and developing processes the potency of nature's germens. Shakespeare has absorbed the idea and permits it to serve as the concentration point of his demonic metaphysics in *Macbeth*.

## II

Macbeth conjures the Witches by those powers which they profess to exert:

> Though you untie the winds and let them fight
> Against the churches; though the yesty waves
> Confound and swallow navigation up;
> Though bladed corn be lodged and trees blown down;
> Though castles topple on their warders' heads;
> Though palaces and pyramids do slope
> Their heads to their foundations; though the treasure
> Of Nature's germens tumble all together,
> Even till destruction sicken: answer me
> To what I ask you. (*Macbeth,* IV, i, 56–65)

The *Natures Germaine,* or germain, of the Folios have, in other editions, been made to read *natures germains, german, nature's germins, germens.* This variety of readings has led to quite diverse interpretations of the passage. For example, Elwin says: 'Nature's *german* are *nature's kindred*—that is, *mankind in general. The treasure of nature's german,* is, therefore, the best of the human race.' According to R. G. White, 'Germins are sprouting seeds. The word is here used in the largest figurative sense.' Theobald, in a note to *Lear,* III, ii, 8, says: 'Mr. Pope has explained Germains to mean *relations,* or *kindred* Elements. Then it must have been *germanes* (from the Latin, *germanus*). But the poet here means "spill all the *Seeds of Matter,* that are hoarded within it." To retrieve which Sense we must write *Germins;* and so we must again in *Macbeth.* And to put this Emendation beyond all Doubt, I'll produce one more Passage, where our Author not only uses the same Thought again, but the word that ascertains my Explication. In *Winter's Tale,* IV, iv, 490, "Let Nature crush the sides o' the Earth together, And marr the *Seeds* within." ' [1] And Professor Hardin Craig notes: '*Nature's germens,* seeds or elements, from which nature operates.' [2] It is the purpose of this chapter to expand Theobald's idea that *Nature's germens* are 'seeds of matter' by reference to the conception in mediaeval metaphysics of the *rationes seminales,* or *logoi spermatikoi,* which in this passage Shakespeare probably had in mind. The power of demons to order and develop *rationes seminales* and the significance of this conception in an understanding of the demonic metaphysics of *Macbeth* will be noticed.

31

From the Stoics and Neo-Platonists on down to Shakespeare philosophers and scientists undertook in various ways to explain the mysterious, generative powers of nature—its qualities, manner of functioning, and ultimate source. According to the Stoics, the cyclic generation and destruction of the world is regulated by a necessity involving a natural and inviolable law of cause and effect. This all-producing and directing Law is always rational in its activities and is, accordingly, called Destiny or Reason of the World. In its capacity of creating the forms of nature, however, this universal Reason is called the *logos spermatikos,* or Creative Reason. This *logos spermatikos* is the power which, acting according to an inner law, produces all things from 'primary fire as from a seed,' gives them form and shape, life, and (in the case of man) reason and all the activities of the soul. It represents the 'creative and forming forces in nature, which have collectively produced the universe, and particular exercises of which produce individual things;—it is at once *material,* the material germ of things, and *form,* the law which determines their shape and qualities.'[3] Marcus Aurelius defines this celebrated term as 'certain germs of future existences, endowed with productive capacities of realization, change, and phenomenal succession.'[4] Here is one explanation of the 'seeds of matter.'

The Neo-Platonists, on the other hand, while taking over the term, gave it a quite different connotation. According to Plotinus, says Dean Inge, the world of sense is created by the Universal Soul through the instrumentality of Nature 'which is its moving power . . . its active faculty . . . its expansion of energy. On the other hand Nature is also the activity of Matter; it is that which, added to Matter, gives it its substantiality. . . . It is the lowest of the spiritual existences . . . unconscious, but casts upon Matter a reflexion of the forms which it has received from above. . . . The thoughts of the Soul are not ideas but *logoi,* creative powers,' and through these nature creates the four elements and all the things of the world of sense.[5] Says Plotinus:

It is the Reason which produces in matter; but the principle that produces naturally is neither a thought nor an intuition, but a power that fashions matter unconsciously. . . . The Soul produces by the forms. The forms she transmits are by her received from the Intelligence. This Intelligence, however, gives the forms to the Universal Soul which is located immediately below her, and the Universal Soul transmits them to the inferior soul (the natural generative power), fashioning and illuminating her. The inferior soul then produces. . . . As she has received the power of production, and she contains the reasons which are not the first (the 'seminal reasons,' which are inferior to the Ideas) not only does she, by virtue of what she has received, produce, but she also draws from herself something which is evidently inferior (matter).[6]

These creative powers, *logoi spermatikoi,* which Nature receives as impressions and casts upon Matter, represent still another conception of the 'seeds of matter.' Now combining certain elements of the Stoical and Neo-Platonic ideas regarding the *logoi spermatikoi* and transforming them to suit his own theology, St. Augustine evolved his theory of Exemplarism, which remained popular throughout the Middle Ages and into the Renaissance.

### III

Augustine's exemplarism is advanced in explanation of the relationship between God and his creation. According to Augustine God's knowledge of his own Essence makes it possible for him to visualize all the finite essences which are capable of being realized outside of himself and which are but frail resemblances of aspects of his Essence. Thus before any essence is created in the actual world it exists in God as an *exemplar,* or *idea,* or *ratio,* or *regula.* And when he came to create the world of contingent things, he made selections from these types or ideas and objectified them in pale imitations, which constitute the things of sense. First he created out of nothing a chaotic mass, called prime matter, impregnated with the germs of all created things, *rationes seminales.* These *rationes seminales* represent the material essences which correspond to the exemplars in God's mind.[7] In this discussion we are interested primarily

34

in the *rationes seminales*. Augustine says: 'But, in truth, some hidden seeds of all things that are born corporeally and visibly, are concealed in the corporeal elements of this world. For those seeds that are now visible to our eyes from fruits and living things, are quite distinct from the hidden seeds of those former seeds; from which at the bidding of the Creator, the water produced the first swimming creatures and fowl, and the earth the first buds after their kind, and the first living creatures after their kind. For neither at that time were those seeds so drawn forth into products of their several kinds, as that the power of production was exhausted in those products; but oftentimes, suitable combinations of circumstances are wanting, whereby they may be enabled to burst forth and complete their species.[8] For consider, the very least shoot is a seed; for, if fitly consigned to the earth, it will produce a tree. But of this shoot there is yet a more subtle seed in the grain of the same species, and this is visible even to us. But of this grain also there is further still a seed, which, although we are unable to see it with our eyes, yet we can conjecture its existence from our reason; because, except there were some such power in those elements, there would not so frequently be produced from the earth things which had not been sown there. . . . For the Creator of these invisible seeds is the Creator of all things himself; since whatever comes forth to our sight by being born, receives the first beginnings of its course from hidden seeds, and takes the successive increments of its proper size and its distinctive forms from these as it were original rules.' [9] Thus God creates continuously from within, has created already within prime matter the germs of all possible visible things in the world. But the exterior operations of nature depend upon suitable combinations of circumstances or perhaps upon the activities of good or bad men or angels. But more of that anon. For the present it is sufficient to point out that the *rationes seminales* of the Augustinian conception represent adequately, I believe, the *nature's germens* of Shakespeare's *Macbeth*.

It does not seem necessary here to trace in detail the transmission of this doctrine throughout the Middle Ages and into the Renaissance. We may examine, however, some significant, if slight, modifications of it. St. Anselm, for example, is practically in agreement with Augustine on the matter of exemplarism: 'Patet itaque quoniam priusquam fierent universa, erat in ratione summae naturae, quid aut qualia aut quomodo futura essent. . . .' [10] Quod quoniam aliter esse non potest, nisi ut ea, quae facta, per aliud vigeant, et id a quo facta sunt, vigeat per seipsum, necesse est ut sicut nihil factum est nisi per creatricem praesentem essentiam.' [11] St. Bonaventure conceives of prime matter as being, not pure passivity, but endowed with a reality of its own, a desire to complete a series of forms in agreement with nature, and a vital power of realizing these desires. It carries these forms and powers within itself as *rationes seminales*. 'The *ratio seminalis* is an incomplete but active germ, an interior energy which in every substantial transformation works together with external agents—*movet et operatur ad effectus productionem.*' [12] The celebrated Dominican, Robert Kilwardby, defines the term: 'Evolutio illarum rationum et explicatio per res actuales fit per secula, materia naturalis prima . . . est quid dimensiones habens corporeas, impregnatum originalibus rationibus sive potentiis ex quibus procendi sunt actus omnium specificorum corporum.' [13] His successor, Archbishop Peckham, urges a return to various doctrines of Augustine . . . 'que quicquid docet Augustinus de regulis a eternis . . . de rationibus seminalibus inditis materiae'; [14] and Albert the Great makes the *rationes seminales* an integral part of his system.[15] Roger Bacon postulates a *materia universalis*, from which all bodies are produced, which has deposited in it certain *rationes seminales* together with an active appetite urging through successive stages their complete realization. Thus nature is, in one sense, active—*materia est causa alietatis*; [16] but it is passive in the sense that external forces may be instrumental in actuating its potentialities.[17]

Thomas Aquinas, on the other hand, opposes the doctrine that prime matter has within it a latent treasury of forces which determine the later development of things. He supports rather the hylomorphic theory of substantial transformation, holding that corporeal matter is pure undetermined passivity, capable, however, of changing in proportion as it realizes under external stimulus a succession of new forms.[18] Having established this fundamental principle, he is at considerable pains to harmonize it with Augustine's theory of *ratio seminalis,* which (in accordance with his usual attitude of being unwilling to contradict the Bishop of Hippo) he does not wish to abandon altogether. He accepts, therefore, the theory of *ratio seminalis* when applied to the generation of living things. Says he: 'Now in the whole corporeal nature, living bodies are the most perfect: wherefore the word *nature* has been transferred from living things to all natural things. For the word, *nature,* . . . was first applied to signify the generation of living things, which is called *nativity:* and because living things are generated from a principle united to them, as fruit from a tree, and the offspring from the mother, to whom it is united, consequently the word *nature* has been applied to every principle of movement existing in that which is moved. Now it is manifest that the active and passive principles of the generation of living things are the seeds from which things are generated. Therefore Augustine fittingly gave the name *rationes seminales* to all those active and passive virtues which are the principles of natural generation and movement.' [19] He finds that these

38

active and passive virtues may be considered in several ways: 'In the first place, as Augustine says, they are primarily and originally in the Word of God as *typal ideas*. Secondly, they are in the elements of the world, where they were produced altogether at the beginning, as in *universal causes*. Thirdly, they are in those things which, in the succession of time, are produced by universal causes, for instance in this plant, and in that animal, as in particular causes. Fourthly, they are in the seeds produced from animals and plants.' [20] He concludes, therefore, that these active and passive virtues of natural things, 'etsi non possint dici *rationes* secundum quod sunt in materia corporali,' may be called *virtues* in respect of their origin, forasmuch as they are the effect of *rationes ideales*.[21]

It is not surprising to find that the notion of *rationes seminales*, seeds of matter, the active and passive principles of nature, should still have persisted in that strange mélange of conflicting philosophies which characterizes the Renaissance. Experiments were being instituted which should later lead to discovery of the laws of nature; but in the humanistic period most natural philosophers still preferred to juggle with the ancient occult virtues, the treasury of latent forces in nature, in an effort to penetrate the mysteries about them.[22] Neo-Platonism and natural magic were particularly instrumental in perpetuating the doctrine of *rationes seminales*.

Iamblichus, for example, comments upon the infinite powers of the celestial Gods and concludes:

The last genus of all the powers in them is physical. But again, of this power one portion being inherent in spermatic reasons, and prior to these reasons being established in immovable natures, essentially precedes generation.[23]

Marsilius Ficinus edits and translates the *Enneads* of Plotinus, thus introducing to the Renaissance the conception of *rationes seminales* as unconscious creative forces in nature.[24] Henry Cornelius Agrippa bases his whole philosophy of natural magic upon the idea of occult virtues infused into all things:

Platonists say that all inferior bodies are exemplified by the superior *Ideas*. Now they define an *Idea* to be a form, above bodies, souls, minds, and to be one, simple, pure, immutable . . . and eternal; and that the nature of all *Ideas* in the first place is in the very Goodness itself (*i.e.*), God, by way of cause. . . . In the second place, they place them in the very Intelligible Itself (*i.e.*) in the *Soul of the World*, differing the one from the other by absolute forms, so that all the *Ideas* in God indeed are but one form, but in the Soul of the World there are many. . . . They place them in Nature, as certain small Seeds of Forms infused by the *Ideas*, and lastly they place them in matter, as Shadows. Hereunto may be added, that in the Soul of the World there be as many Seminal Forms of things as *Ideas* in the mind of God, by which forms she did in the heavens above the Stars frame to herself shapes also, and stamped upon all these some properties. On these Stars, therefore, shapes and properties, all virtues of inferior species . . . do depend; so that every species hath its Celestial Shape, or figure that is suitable to it, from which also proceeds a wonderful power of *operating,* which proper gift it receives from its own *Idea,* through the Seminal Forms of the Soul of the World.[25]

Even the scientist and philosopher, Francis Bacon, can still believe in an ancient and honorable sort of magic defined as 'that science, which leads to the knowledge of hidden forms, for producing great effects, and by joining agents to patients setting the capital works of nature to view'; [26] and in his experiments he is still searching for the seeds of things: 'Etiam semina rerum potestate valida, usu (nisi processu suo) nihili sunt.' [27] And as late as 1652 Ashmole explains that in the magical generation of frogs, lice and worms

The worke of a *Philosopher* is therein onely to strengthen the *Seeds of Nature,* (for she alone Workes) and so to quicken them that they hasten the worke of *Generation* (and by such meanes *Tho. Aquinas* supposes *Pharos Magitians* produced *Froggs*) insomuch as it seems to the *Ignorant* not to be the *Worke of Nature,* (that usually operates more leasurely) rather the *Power* of the *Devill.*[28]

Enquiry into the immediate source of Shakespeare's 'nature's germens' is as futile as unprofitable. The conception of germs in prime matter or in living substance was so well known to philosophers of the Middle Ages and the Renaissance that it would have been most strange had he not heard of it. He might have received instruction on the matter from the teachings of Augustine or of Thomas Aquinas, or he might have investigated some work on occult philosophy with a Neo-Platonic or Stoic impression upon it. Apparently almost any idea promulgated in the world before had a good chance of being reproduced and criticized in the Renaissance. More significant for a study of *Macbeth* is the fact that Shakespeare has associated nature's germens with a demonic power of the Weird Sister to tumble these seeds of matter all together, or otherwise manipulate them, until destruction sicken. In this he may well be following the Augustinian tradition.

IV

Augustine's discussion of the *rationes seminales* occurs in connection with his estimate of the power of demons—and through them, of magicians—to work miracles. He demonstrates, of course, that only God is the true creator of the universe and the worker of miracles, *i.e.,* effects produced against nature or above nature. We have already seen how whatever comes forth to our sight by being born received the first beginnings of its course from hidden seeds which the Creator placed in prime matter, but the development of these *rationes seminales* may, by permission of God, be subject to the power and will of demons. 'So in the creation of visible things it is God that works from within; but the exterior operations, whether good or bad, of angels or men, or even of any kind of animal, according to his own absolute power, and to the distribution of faculties, and the several appetites for things pleasant, which He himself has imparted, are applied by him to that nature of things wherein He created all things.' [29] When demons, therefore, produce effects by perfectly natural means that seem so marvelous as to approach the miraculous, no one must suppose that they are performing real miracles. Says Augustine:

As, therefore, we do not call parents the creators of men, nor farmers the creators of corn—although it is by the outward application of their actions that the power of God operates within for the creating of these things—so it is not right to think not only the bad but even the good angels to be creators, if, through the subtility of their perception and body, they know the seeds of things which to us are more hidden, and scatter them secretly through fit temperings of the elements, and so furnish opportunities of producing things, and of accelerating their increase. . . .

For all these things in the way of origin and beginning have already been created in a kind of texture of the elements, but they come forth when they have opportunity. For as mothers are pregnant with young, so the world itself is pregnant with the causes of things that are born. . . . But the applying from without of adventitious causes, which, although they are not natural, yet are to be applied according to nature, in order that those things which are contained in the secret bosom of nature may break forth and be out-

43

wardly created in some way by the unfolding of the proper measures and numbers and weights which they have received in secret from Him—this is not only in the power of bad angels, but also of bad men.[30]

In other words, whatever things may be produced by the regular processes of nature, may—if God permits it—be developed instantly or at will by demons, who know the seeds of matter and are able to handle them as they please. They have the power of tumbling nature's germens all together even till destruction sicken.

Thomas Aquinas accepts, with reservations, and rationalizes Augustine's demonic metaphysics. He also is of the opinion that 'spiritual powers are able to effect whatever happens in this visible world, by employing corporeal seeds by local movement.'[31] It must not be supposed, however, that corporeal matter obeys the will of demons to the extent that they are able to transmute matter from one form to another. 'But they can employ certain seeds that exist in the elements of the world in order to produce these effects, as Augustine says. Therefore it must be admitted that all the transformations of corporeal things which can be produced by certain natural powers, to which we must assign the seeds above mentioned, can alike be produced by the operation of demons, by the employment of these seeds; such as the transformation of certain things into serpents or frogs, which can be produced by putrefaction. On the contrary, those transformations which cannot be produced by the power of nature, cannot in reality be effected by the operation of demons; for instance, that the human body be changed into the body of a beast, or that the body of a dead man return to life.' [32] He insists, however, that there are active and passive virtues in certain parts of corporeal things, 'and when they are employed with local movement for the production of certain results, we speak of demons as employing seeds.' [33] Moreover, when Augustine says, 'As a mother is pregnant with the unborn offspring, so is the world itself pregnant with the causes of unborn things,' Aquinas concludes that these seminal virtues may also be considered as causal virtues, just as seed is a kind of cause, remembering always that the ultimate causal virtues are the typal ideas.[34] Therefore, demons, understanding and controlling the active and passive principles of generated things, may be said to have power over the causes of things. This distinction is important when we come to consider the clairvoyance of demons and their knowledge of the future. And whatever powers demons possess may be acquired by magicians through 'private contract.' [35]

Now just what relation precisely, it may be enquired, does the demonic intelligence bear to time—present, past, and future? Shakespeare must have had this question in mind when he made Banquo also conjure the Weird Sisters:

If you can look into the seeds of time,
And say which grain will grow and which will not,
Speak then to me. (*Macbeth*, I, iii, 58–60)

Their reply indicates that they have a clear vision of
the present and a certain knowledge of the future:
'Thou shalt get kings, though thou be none.' Thomas
Aquinas explains fully the metaphysical knowledge
which demons—or men through the aid of demons—
may have of the present and the future. He finds that
the angelic knowledge of truth is twofold: 'One which
comes of nature, and one which comes of grace.' [36] Of
these two sorts of knowledge, the first was neither
taken away nor lessened in the demons. 'For it follows
from the very nature of the angel, who, according to
his nature, is an intellect or mind: since on account
of the simplicity of his substance, nothing can be
withdrawn from his nature, so as to punish him by
subtracting from his natural powers. . . . Consequently, their knowledge was not diminished' (I. 64.
1. c.). Since it is the prerogative of the angelic nature to administer things here below (I. 57. 2. c.), naturally 'the demons know what happens outwardly
among men' (I. 114. 2, *ad* 2). This is possible because
'angels know singulars by universal forms, which
nevertheless are images of things both as to their
universal, and as to their individuating principles'
(I. 57. 2, *ad* 3). That is to say, demons know things not
only by reason of the subtlety of their natures but
also 'by long experience; not as deriving it from the

senses; but when the similitude of their innate intelligible species is completed in individual things, they know things as present, which they did not previously know would come to pass' (I. 64. 1, *ad* 5). Therefore, all 'present things have a nature according to which they resemble the species in the mind of an angel; and so they can be known thereby' (I. 57. 3, *ad* 3). They cannot, however, know the inward disposition of a man's mind except as they are able to make inferences from occult bodily modifications.

It may be thought that the demons, since they are created intelligences, know indifferently the present, past, and future, that their minds are above time. This is not true; only God knows the future in the sense that He sees all things 'in His eternity, which being simple, is present to all time, and embraces all time' (I. 57. 3. c.). But any created intelligence is above that time which is the measure of the movement of corporeal things (I. 85. 4, *ad* 1). Therefore, says Thomas Aquinas, 'The future can be known in two ways. First, it can be known in its causes. And thus, future events which proceed necessarily from their causes, are known with sure knowledge; as that the sun will rise tomorrow. But events which proceed from their causes in the majority of cases, are not known for certain, but conjecturally; thus the doctor knows beforehand the health of his patient. This manner of knowing the future events exists in the angels, and by so much the more than it does in us, as they

47

understand the causes of things both more universally and more perfectly. . . . But events which proceed from their causes in the minority of cases are quite unknown; such as casual and chance events' (I. 57. 3. c.). In this sense, the demons, having lost nothing of their angelic nature, know the future development of events conjecturally though not absolutely. As we have seen, they know the causes of things, in the sense that the *rationes seminales* may be called the causal virtues from which all things are created. They not only understand the seeds of things but are able to scatter them through fit temperings of the elements and so furnish opportunities of producing things and of accelerating their increase. If time is the measure of movement of corporeal things and if corporeal things move and develop according to the impulses latent in that treasury of forces called *rationes seminales,* then these seeds of matter may literally be called the seeds of time and demons have the power of predicting which grain will grow and which will not.

In conclusion, it may be remarked that this study is not concerned with the discovery of definite sources for Shakespeare's nature's germens; it does sketch briefly the development of an idea and its transmission from the Middle Ages to the Renaissance. It suggests that the Shakespearean term is profoundly metaphysical and that it may be conceived as equivalent to Augustine's *ratio seminalis* or the Stoic or Neo-Platonic *logos spermatikos*. But whether Shakespeare considered this treasury of latent forces as producing the phenomena of the inorganic as well as of the organic world of sense cannot be precisely determined. I have assumed that the Weird Sisters are not ordinary witches—which is self-evident—but popular, dramatic symbols of the demonic metaphysics which penetrates the inmost actions of the drama. And the fact that he associates the idea of 'seeds of matter' with the power of demons to know the causes of things and manipulate them, seems to indicate that he may be following the Augustinian tradition in some form. At any rate, this study may serve as a sort of introduction to a fuller discussion of the metaphysics of evil in *Macbeth,* the pattern of which seems to be definitely mediaeval.[37]

*Nec color ullus erat rebus, tene-
brisque malignis:
Et coelum & terras nox circumfusa
tenebat.*

GIOVANNI PONTANO

# Chapter III

## THE DEMONIC METAPHYSICS OF MACBETH *

### I

As dramatic symbols, Shakespeare's Weird Sisters seem to be pre-eminently adequate and successful. In appearance, speech, and action they seem intended to suggest accurately such witches and witchcraft as were familiar to the Elizabethan public. They are desiccated, hag-like creatures with choppy fingers, skinny lips, and beards, who dwell preferably in the murk of desert places and rejoice in upheavals of nature. Upon occasion, indeed, they themselves brew storms on land and tempests at sea, thus destroying the products of men's hands at home and distressing or sinking ships abroad. Their sail-boats are sieves. Associated with them in ceremonial dances—conducted under the influence of the magic number three and its multiples—are evil spirits in the form of cats and toads or sometimes in the likeness of a woman; they employ parts of dismembered dead bodies, toads, and adders in winding up their necromantic charms.

* This chapter appeared first in N. C. *Studies in Philology*, XXX (1933), 395–426.

Compacts with the devil and his angels assure them a certain prophetic power, though they are likely to accomplish their ends by means of half-truths. All the hocus-pocus of magic rites seems to be familiar to them. And such, we are told,[1] is the very form and fashion of Elizabethan witches. Like all fully sufficient dramatic symbols, they may be described as being true to nature. But, as most critics are agreed, they are not merely witches.

There is a curious majesty and even sublimity about the wayward creatures who meet Macbeth and Banquo upon the heath that is not at all characteristic of ordinary witches. Among them they seem to know the past, present, and something of the future; they possess the power of vanishing like bubbles into thin air. Holinshed speaks of 'three women in strange and wild apparell, resembling creatures of elder world . . . either the weird sisters, that is (as ye would say) the goddesses of destinie, or else some nymphs or feiries, indued with knowledge of prophesie by their necromanticall science.' For some of Shakespeare's critics his Weird Sisters seem to have properties in common with Urda, Verdandi, and Skulda, the Nornae of Scandinavian mythology;[2] for others they suggest the classical Parcae or the enchantress, Circe.[3] Possibly Shakespeare's figures are all of these and more.[4] The symbols through which a great dramatic artist concretes his abstract thought

54

are never simple. They are usually immensely complex and therefore the more stimulating, compounded out of many contradictory elements, assimilated and fused by the artistic imagination into a unified whole. Thus the Weird Sisters of earlier scenes and the evidently vulgar witches who appear later are merely different elements, or views, or aspects of the same dramatic symbol. They possess in their own right a certain dignity and mysterious quality which inspires awe in the beholder and compels contemplation. But the wise man will not limit his attention to the symbol as such, however fascinating it may be. He will submit himself fully to its influence, without doubt, but with the idea of achieving through it an aesthetic experience as nearly like that of the author as possible. In other words, he will recognize that the function of the dramatic symbol is to stimulate his imagination to the point of grasping some underlying emotional, moral, or intellectual content.

II

That the Weird Sisters possess in this capacity a perennial and astounding vitality is attested by the whole sweep of Shakespearean criticism. All hands seem to be convinced that they symbolize or represent evil in its most malignant form, though there is to be found little unanimity of opinion regarding the precise nature of that evil, whether it is subjective or objective or both, whether mental or metaphysical. For example, modernists will have it that the Weird Sisters are nothing more than the objectification upon the stage of Macbeth's evil passions and desires;[5] 'They are simply the embodiment of inward temptation; they come in storm and vanish in air, like corporeal impulses, which, originating in the blood, cast up bubbles of sin and ambition in the soul.'[6] One man finds that these 'repulsive things . . . are here a symbol of the hostile powers which operate in nature';[7] and another is of the opinion that 'theirs is an independent vitality of evil whirling through the universe till it finds asylum in the soul where germs of sin lie ready to be quickened to life.'[8] Bradley supposes that they 'must represent not only the evil slumbering in the hero's soul, but all those obscurer influences of evil around him in the world which . . . are as certain, momentous, and terrifying facts as the presence of inchoate evil in the soul itself.'[9] They have at various times been characterized as concrete symbols of that element of negation and destructiveness that is opposed to all order and growth,[10] spirits of evil in its most malignant form, the materialization of a spiritual cosmos of evil,[11] Macbeth's crime nightmare projected into action,[12] limbs of Satan,[13] representatives of hellish Power,[14] infernal spirits,[15] and demons.[16] For Pastor Moritz Petri they seem to symbolize 'a secret world of evil

56

spirits that with Satanic cunning lie in wait for human souls, conquering the unguarded heart and rejoicing in hurling their victim to the dust in the misery of sin. Under this weight of demoniac influences lies Macbeth when the drama opens.' [17] One cannot help observing, while reviewing criticisms of Shakespeare's *Macbeth*, that these commentators have been excited and stimulated, through the instrumentality of powerful dramatic symbols, to achieve imaginatively some sort of marvellous experience. Each exuberantly interprets the symbol according to his nature and ways of thinking; each creates, in a measure, and possesses his own *Macbeth* and proceeds to tell the world about it with enthusiasm. This is precisely as it should be. Indeed, each is so enamored of his own experience and so delighted with his proper *Macbeth* that he is likely to conclude: Such and no other must have been Shakespeare's *Macbeth*. This is perhaps understandable but not as it should be. For some lack adequate knowledge of the Elizabethan age and so are unable to experience the full effects of the stimuli which urged Shakespeare to create; others are so immersed in the possible stimuli of the age that they can recognize little beyond dramatic symbols as such. Shakespeare's *Macbeth* still is, and no doubt must always remain, a mystery. But the flood of *Macbeths* created and described by a host of critics still bears witness to the efficacy of his dramatic symbols.

57

III

Now the present writer offers no criticism either of Shakespeare's *Macbeth* or of his own; it would be difficult, therefore, for what he has to say to be brought into conflict with the work of Shakespeare's critics. He has perhaps possessed his own *Macbeth*, but the experience is not revealed here. The single purpose of this study is to examine, as thoroughly as possible, the nature of that evil which the Weird Sisters are said to symbolize or represent, and to reproduce one aspect at least of the metaphysical groundwork of the drama. It presupposes that in Shakespeare's time evil was considered to be both subjective and, so far as the human mind is concerned, a non-subjective reality; that is to say, evil manifested itself subjectively in the spirits of men and objectively in a metaphysical world whose existence depended in no degree upon the activities of the human mind. This objective realm of evil was not governed by mere vague and irrational forces; it was peopled and controlled by the malignant wills of intelligences— evil spirits, devils, demons, Satan—who had the ability to project their power into the workings of nature and to influence the human spirit. Such a system of evil was raised to the dignity of a science and a theology. The wisest of men—with the exception of a small minority who, like Bruno, sat in the seats of the

Sadducees—believed in the world of evil spirits: Sir Matthew Hale, Bishop Hall, Richard Baxter, Dr. Henry More, Dr. Willis, Glanville, Lavater, Sir Thomas Browne, Catholics and Protestants alike, physicians, philosophers, theologians, Kings.[18] Even the scientist, Sir Francis Bacon, classifies knowledge of angels and unclean spirits under Natural Theology, and concludes:

The same is to be understood of revolted or unclean spirits: conversation with them, or using their assistance, is unlawful; and much more in any manner to worship or adore them: but the contemplation and knowledge of their nature, power, and illusions, appears from Scripture, reason, and experience, to be no small part of spiritual wisdom.[19]

And that skeptic and militant Calvinist, Reginald Scot, while opposing the Sadducees on the one hand and the Neo-Platonists on the other, confesses with Augustine that these matters are above his capacity:

And yet so farre as Gods word teacheth me, I will not sticke to saie, that they are living creatures, ordeined to serve the estate, yet that they are the Lords ministers, and executioners of his wrath, to trie and tempt in this world, and to punish the reprobate in hell fier in the world to come.[20]

Since, then, this belief was so universal at the time, we may reasonably suppose that Shakespeare's Weird Sisters are intended to symbolize or represent the metaphysical world of evil spirits. Whether one considers them as human witches in league with the powers of darkness, or as actual demons in the form of witches, or as merely inanimate symbols, the power which they wield or represent or symbolize is ultimately demonic. Let us, therefore, exercise wisdom in the contemplation of the nature, power, and illusions of unclean spirits.

In the meantime, we may conveniently assume that in essence the Weird Sisters are demons or devils in the form of witches. At least their control over the primary elements of nature, the *rationes seminales*, would seem to indicate as much.[21] Why, then, should Shakespeare have chosen to present upon his stage these witch-likenesses rather than devils in devil-forms? Two equally valid reasons may be suggested. In the first place, the rather sublime devil and his angels of the earlier drama, opponents of God in the cosmic order and destroyers of men, had degenerated in the hands of later dramatists into mere comic figures; by Shakespeare's time folk conception[22] had apparently so dominated dramatic practice and tradition that cloven hoof, horns, and tail became associated in the popular imagination only with the ludicrous. As Whitmore says: 'We thus see that devil-plays after *Faustus* progress steadily in the direction of comedy, a movement which reaches its logical conclusion in the monumental humours of Jonson's *The Devil is an Ass.*'[23] For Shakespeare's audience, therefore, the presentation of actual devils upon the stage could suggest only dimly, if at all, the terror

60

and sublimity of a metaphysical world of evil. In the second place, witches had acquired no such comic associations. They were essentially tragic beings who, for the sake of certain abnormal powers, had sold themselves to the devil. As we have seen, everybody believed in them as channels through which the malignity of evil spirits might be visited upon human beings. Here, then, were terrifying figures, created by a contemporary public at the most intense moment of witchcraft delusion, which Shakespeare found ready to his hand. Accordingly he appropriately employed witch-figures as dramatic symbols, but the Weird Sisters are in reality demons, actual representatives of the world of darkness opposed to good.[24]

## IV

But of precisely what class or order or system of demons they are representatives is a profoundly vexing question. The Renaissance, with its apparently omnivorous appetite for the occult, welcomes its demons from every quarter of the universe and herds them into a chaos and confusion resembling that of Pandemonium. Here the devils of popular folk superstition, created in the imaginations of many peoples by terror of the unknown, rub shoulders with the demons of many respectable philosophical systems and with the fallen angels of Christian theology. As Postellus remarks: 'In nulla re major fuit altercatio,

61

major obscuritas, minor opinionum concordia, quam de daemonibus et substantiis separatis.' [25] Here appear again the monstrous offspring of Adam and Lilith,[26] consorting with the progeny of wayward sons of God and the seductively fair daughters of men [27] and the spawn of incubi and succubi.[28] Pythagorean souls of departed good and wicked men, cherished and perpetuated by the Stoics, still flit about the earth, persecuting or ministering to mortals; [29] Socrates' good daemon and Plato's sons of gods by nymphs or other mothers, intermediaries between men and gods,[30] meet themselves after centuries transformed and fused with the Roman genius or with the creatures of the Neo-Platonic imagination.[31] Christianity brings to the Renaissance all the gods of ancient paganism,[32] together with the malignant powers of conquered heathenism,[33] metamorphosed into devils and demons. And the legions of devils, a third part of all the angels of heaven who fell with Lucifer when he fell, still lord it over hell and the regions of the earth.[34] Elizabethan England is acquainted with an infinite variety of demons: eudaemons and cacodaemons, rulers of the planets, demons of fire, air, water, earth, and spaces under the earth; aristocratic and plebeian devils; legions of devils that come when called by name with incantations and suffumigations to serve men in evil capacities; demons corporeal and incorporeal, that take what shapes they please. As Burton says:

They will have no place void but full of Spirits, Devils, and other inhabitants. . . . Not so much as an hair breadth empty in heaven, earth, or waters, above or under the earth. The air is not so full of flies in summer, as it is at all times of invisible spirits.[35]

Thus philosophy, theology, and religion have joined themselves with theosophy,[36] theurgy, and thaumaturgy,[37] with superstitious legend, classical and folk mythology, black magic and other occult sciences, in creating for the Renaissance mind a spiritual world of evil intelligences. And each demonic system seems to be colored, to some extent, by constant interplay of influences between itself and other systems.

## v

In spite of the astounding disorder in Renaissance classifications of demons, however, the thoughtful student must recognize in them the outlines of at least two important systems of philosophy, namely, the Neo-Platonic and the Christian. He will recall that in the complicated history of philosophy human minds have set themselves to solve the problem of God's relation to his universe, a problem involving the contradiction between God's Oneness and the world's heterogeneity, the dualism between spirit and substance, good and evil. In the attempt to conciliate these extremes, there have evolved two systems of cosmology, creationism and emanationism, each of

which employs a series of mediators to bridge the
chasm between God and the world. On the one hand,
Neo-Platonism, as best represented in the works of
Plotinus, conceives of the world as emanating from
God through three successive spheres of activity:
First, there is God the Absolute, the transcendent
One, undetermined, unchangeable in essence, and
plural only in his workings. This first principle of
divine activity expresses itself 'according to the necessity of its essence' in a second sphere called Rational Spirit (νοῦς), which is differentiated into the
duality of thought and being; this Rational Spirit
causes to emanate from itself Universal Soul (ψυχή'),
which receives the world of Ideas from Spirit and uses
them as archetypes after which it, as active principle,
creates the cosmos, or world of sense. From Soul,
therefore, proceeds the formative power of Nature
(φύσις) and individual souls. Now from the World
Soul emanate the bright gods; and from nature emanate daemons. Thus the divine power of God is lik-
ened to Light, which shines into the darkness and de-
creases in intensity in proportion to the distance from
the source until it is finally swallowed up in darkness.
The ultimate darkness in which this Light loses itself
is Matter (ὕλη), the opposite and negation of Spirit,
therefore Evil. 'Evil is not itself something positively
existent; it is want or deficiency; it is lack of Good,
Non-being.' [38] Daemons may be said to represent the
ultimate scattering forth of Spirit activities; they are

the lower order of divine beings whose sphere of activity is below the spiritual world. They are 'powers proceeding from the Soul as a dweller on earth; their power is confined to the region "below the moon." They are everlasting and can behold the spiritual world above them; but they have bodies of "spiritual matter," and can clothe themselves in fiery or airy integuments; they can feel and remember, and hear petitions.' [39] It is quite clear that the human soul intent upon absorption back into the Absolute must pass in reverse through these successive spheres of activity, and it can reach the realm of the gods above the moon only by climbing first the ladder represented by the hierarchy of daemonic powers. Daemons are, therefore, necessary mediators between gods and men; they are divine beings who look upon the spiritual world, though they cannot inhabit it, and reveal its mysteries to human beings.

This spiritual doctrine of the nature and function of daemons is debased by later Neo-Platonists into a fantastic system of mythology and theurgy. In the hands of Porphyry, Iamblichus, Proclus, and Olympiodorus the number of stages through which the Absolute streams forth the world is increased; the gods of various religions are absorbed and accommodated in the system; [40] good and evil spirits of the Persians, Jews, Chaldees, Greeks and Romans, and the demons of folk belief are welcomed somewhere within the six ranks of Neo-Platonic sublunary daemons. These divine powers are no longer to be merely worshiped; they may under certain circumstances be coerced by the will of man to accomplish wonders for his satisfaction. Thus the philosophy of Plotinus has degenerated into a species of magic. Though the Neo-Platonic cosmology is well known to the Renaissance, I cannot find any evidence that Shakespeare's Weird Sisters symbolized the conception of evil which it elaborates.

## VI

Christian philosophy, on the other hand, attempts to explain the relation between God and the world, as well as the origin of evil, by employing the conception of 'free, creative action.' The Original Being is a personality; he created the world in time, not in accordance with the necessity of his essence, but by a supreme act of the creative will. Creation is, therefore, not an eternal process but an accomplished fact; and since the world was created out of nothing by God, it must in the beginning have been universally good. But the fact of evil in the world cannot be ignored. How, then, did evil come into the world of God's creating? Christian philosophy solves the problem of the duality of good and evil by assuming that God originally provided angelic spirits and human souls with a freedom similar to his own and that evil resulted from the opposition of the creature's will to

66

the divine will. Matter, therefore, is not the principle of evil; but the inclination toward matter and the sensuous on the part of free creatures, the bestowal of love upon God's creations rather than upon God himself, constitutes a secondary element in evil. Thus the Christian conception of evil combines the negative element of departure from God, the absence of good, with a positive element involving the rebellion of the perverted finite will against the infinite will.[41] Now Christian philosophy recognizes two tragedies of cosmic importance: (1) The fall of Lucifer and a third part of the angelic hosts, who rebelled against God and were cast out; [42] and (2) the fall of Adam, who was originally endowed with perfection and freedom but who set his will against God's will and so brought sin and limited freedom upon mankind.

A third aspect of the Christian conception of good and evil must not be overlooked, namely, resolution of the spiritual kingdom as if into two diametrically opposed realms, the world of good and the world of evil. Here Christianity acknowledges the influence of Manichaeism, a system of religion based upon Persian mythology and Gnostic belief. According to Mani, it will be remembered, the 'two realms of light and darkness, good and evil, peace and strife, are eternally opposed' the one to the other; and God and Satan, like the ancient Persian Ormazd and Ahriman, rule over these realms respectively.[43] Now when Augustine comes to formulate Christian doctrine, he cannot

quite escape his Manichaean heritage. He accepts evil
as the result of a desire on the part of God's creatures
for absolute self-determination; and since through
Adam's sin all men lost the power of free-choice, only
through God's grace can they be saved from perdi-
tion. His doctrine of predestination destroys man's
free will: God chooses whom he will unto salvation
and unto destruction. For Augustine, says Windelband, 'the whole course of history falls apart into two
spheres—the realm of God and the realm of the devil.
To the former belong the angels that have not fallen,
and the men whom God has chosen for his grace; the
other embraces, together with evil demons, all those
men who are not predestined to redemption . . . ; the
one is the kingdom of heaven, the other that of the
world.' [44] As Windelband concludes: 'Among the
Manichaeans the antithesis of good and evil is held
to be original and indelible; with Augustine this antithesis is regarded as one that has come into being,
but yet one that is ineradicable. The omnipotent,
omniscient, supremely benevolent God has created a
world which is divided forever into his own realm
and that of Satan.' [45] It is precisely this conception of
two worlds which the Renaissance inherits from the
Middle Ages. It is implicit in the Calvin-Arminian
controversy over predestination, in Luther's doctrine
of sin and free grace, and in Catholic theology as
transmitted through the Dominicans, notably through
Thomas Aquinas.[46] It must be emphasized that, for

68

the Middle Ages and for the Renaissance, evil reveals itself in two modes or categories: subjectively as original or other sin in the human spirit, and objectively as the malignant activity of demons or fallen angels. In this study we are not concerned with the inner or subjective aspect of evil. Let us rather inspect the unclean spirits of Christian theology, with the idea of determining their essence, their powers over nature and the spirits of men, and their function in the moral and cosmic orders.

## VII

Now in God's ordering of his created universe, says St. Thomas, we must observe two steps, the 'reason of order' and the 'execution of order.' The type of things ordered toward an end in the mind of God may properly be called Providence; the execution of the providential design is Government. As to the design of government, God governs all things immediately, and nothing escapes from him as universal cause. But in the matter of execution of design, he governs through a mediate chain of secondary causes inherent in the nature of the things created.[47] In this respect God stands outside his universe and intervenes only when he works miracles or extends divine grace to men. Since in the execution of providence inferior things are always governed by superior, there emerges in Christian thinking a hierarchy of causes,

identified for the most part with a chain of superior
and inferior beings, which bridges the chasm between
God and the world. That is to say, the executors of
divine providence are angels, who employ in their
ministry the secondary causes inherent in the natures
of things. Of the angels there are, according to Dionysius, three hierarchies comprising each three orders: In the first hierarchy there are the Seraphim,
Cherubim, and Thrones; in the second, Dominations,
Virtues, and Powers; in the third, Principalities,
Archangels, and Angels.[48] Gregory agrees with this
graduation, except that he places Principalities below
Dominations and above Powers, and Virtues below
Powers and above Archangels.[49] Now regarding their
natures and offices, we may say that the Seraphim ex-
cel all others in that they are united with God himself; 'the Cherubim know the divine secrets'; and
the Thrones know immediately the 'types of things
in God.' Dominations appoint those things which are
to be done; Virtues give the power of execution and
rule over corporeal nature in the working of miracles; Powers order how what has been commanded
can be accomplished, and coerce evil spirits. Principalities and Archangels are the leaders in execution,
and Angels simply perform what is to be done.[50]

According, then, to the 'order of nature the angels
are between God and men, and according to the common law not only human affairs are administered by
them, but also all corporeal matters.'[51] In the corpo-

70

real world, angels exercise control both indirectly and directly: They are the spiritual substances that move the heavenly bodies, *i.e.*, the stars and planets, which in turn govern all the natural operations of inferior bodies on the earth, and they exert an immediate power over those actions of inferior bodies for which the movements of the heavenly bodies are not sufficient explanation.[52] As Augustine says: 'Every visible thing in this world has an angelic power placed over it'; and Origen concludes that 'the world has need of angels who preside over beasts, and over the birth of animals, and over the increase of all other things.'[53] But angels must always bring their regency within the limits prescribed by the natural laws of the things controlled. Thus they may not perform miracles or coerce the wills of men whom they guard.

Now demons, though cast out of heaven, are still spiritual substances; though fallen angels, they are still angels. All their natural powers remain unimpaired; the natural gifts which God bestowed upon them as angels, says Dionysius, 'have not been changed at all, but remain entire and most brilliant.'[54] For example,

The knowledge which comes of nature has neither been taken away nor lessened in the demons. For it follows from the very nature of the angel, who, according to his nature, is an intellect or mind: since on account of the simplicity of his substance, nothing can be withdrawn from his nature, so as to punish him by subtracting from his natural powers.

. . . Consequently, their natural knowledge was not diminished.[55]

In this sense the fallen angels still belong to the original orders of angels from which they fell; and, since the superior rules the inferior, there is precedence and authority among them.[56] Only the knowledge and powers which come of grace are lessened in them. Consequently, these intellectual substances are still superior to that rational substance, man, and may influence him to his destruction or salvation. Indeed, the function of demonic powers in the cosmic order is to participate in the working out of man's destiny. For God in his divine providence so disposes man's welfare that he is 'brought to good and withheld from evil' directly through the offices of good angels. But lest demons should cease to be of service in the natural order, God disposes that they provide opposition to the good in man, so that, through exercise in fighting against evil, the human soul may indirectly be perfected unto salvation. Their place of punishment is two-fold: in hell, where they serve as the executioners of God's wrath upon wicked men; and in the 'darksome atmosphere' of this world,[57] where they act as God's ministers in what Origen calls 'a training school of virtue.'[58] Thus divine Wisdom suffers bad angels to do some evil in the world—but only so much as he permits—for the sake of the good that follows. But he restrains and straitly limits their activities by subjecting them to the coercion of that order of the angelic hierarchy called Powers.[59]

With this limitation of activities in mind, let us look more closely into the demonic nature and powers. Since fallen angels are still intellectual substances or 'subsisting forms, it is impossible for their substances to be corruptible' (I. 50. 5. c.) [60] or to be naturally joined to bodies (I. 51. 1. c.). They recognize and converse with one another through mental concepts, and upon these activities local distance places no restraints (I. 107. 4. c.). They are able to assume bodies of air, condensing it by virtue of their angelic natures insofar as is necessary for the forming of assumed bodies (I. 51. 2, *ad* 3); but these bodies of air are not capable of performing vital functions (I. 51. 3. c.), such as sensation (I. 51. 3, *ad* 6), eating and assimilating food (I. 51. 3, *ad* 5), or reproducing their kind (I. 51. 3, ad 6). 'Properly speaking, demons do not talk through their assumed bodies; yet there is a semblance of speech, insofar as they fashion sounds in the air like human voices,' which may be heard by human ears (I. 51. 3, *ad* 4). As I have shown elsewhere (Ch. II), everything that happens outwardly among men is known to them, not because, like the human mind, they abstract intelligible species of things from them as they unfold, but because the species of things are connatural in spiritual substances. Understanding the

73

causes of things, they know the future development of
events conjecturally though not absolutely. And some
know more than others (I. 55. 3). All of them are clairvoyant, however, their knowledge being 'quite indifferent to what is near or distant'; nevertheless, their
local movements from place to place are not on that account without purpose, because they move from place
to place not to gain knowledge but to act (I. 55. 2, *ad*
3). Their local movements, moreover, are not subject
to the laws governing movement in time which obtain
in the corporeal world. That is to say, 'a daemon's
movement is not continuous; in going from one place
to another he does not necessarily pass through all intermediate places.' His 'substance is not subject to
place as contained thereby, but is above it as containing it; hence it is under his control to apply himself to
any place he wills, either through or without the inter-
vening place' (I. 53. 2. c.). Nor is he subject to that
'time which is the measure of the movement of corporeal things.' A daemon, therefore, can be in one place
in one instant and in another place, say a thousand
miles away, in the next instant without any time inter-
vening (I. 53. 3. c. and *ad* 3). In addition, he can work
apparent miracles in the natural order by the simple
process of manipulating in local movement the seeds
of things; anything that nature can produce through
long or short travail, a demon can achieve instantly
through his knowledge of the active and passive principles of things.[61] He may even intervene in the work-

ing of that law determining that superior bodies govern inferior bodies; since as a spiritual substance he may govern bodies directly, he can work effects independently of the heavenly bodies, such as the creation of tempests and the condensation of the clouds into rain, and such like (I. 110. 1. c, 3. c.; 112. 2. c.).

And finally, demonic powers have the ability to move man's senses and imagination and will, sometimes to his destruction. For the senses can be changed in two ways: 'from without, as when affected by a sensible object; and from within, as when they are affected by disturbed spirits and humours.' Now 'daemons can work a change in the human senses in both ways; they can offer the senses a sensible object from without, formed by nature or by the demons themselves.' Likewise they can move the spirits and humours from within so that the senses are changed in various ways (I. 111. 4. c.). They also move the human imagination. 'Imaginative apparitions are sometimes caused in men by the local movements of spirits and humours,' and daemons by controlling and directing such movements are enabled to induce in the imaginations of men, either waking or asleep, whatever visions and hallucinations they please (I. 111. 3. c.). And they move the human will both by persuasion and by stirring up passions residing in the sensitive appetite. They cannot know the inmost thoughts of the human mind except through interpretation of outward bodily signs; and they cannot plant thoughts in the mind. But they may 'incite to thought' and kindle desire 'by way of persuasion or by rousing the passions' (I. 111. 2, *ad* 2). Thus evil spirits tempt man in two ways: 'first, from within by working on his imagination and senses, so that something seems otherwise than it is. Secondly, from without; for just as they can form from the air a body of any form or shape, and assume it and appear in it visibly: so in the same way can they clothe any corporeal thing with any corporeal form, so as to appear therein' (I. 114. 4, *ad* 2). As we have intimated above, daemons have the will and the power to enter into, and utterly possess, the human body; and they may gain control over the spirit by seizing upon those members in which the vigor of the soul resides.

This outline, then, may be said to represent the demonic metaphysics of Christian theology, which the Renaissance inherits from the Middle Ages. Properly speaking, this is not superstition; even a congenital Methodist, such as the present writer, must recognize that it is a superb rationalization of an almost universal belief incorporated into a logical system of philosophy. Protestant reformers may attack this system in minor or major details; they may go so far as to reduce the principle of evil to the personality of the Devil alone or to personifications of the human vices.[62] But not even Deering, Scot, and Calvin can escape the devil-lore of the Bible; and besides, St. Augustine is always with them.[63] And the Catholic

Church espouses the philosophy of Thomas Aquinas.[64] But whatever may be the Protestant view regarding evil spirits, it seems to be this mediaeval system of metaphysics which manifests itself everywhere in Shakespeare's *Macbeth*.

VIII

For example, in the light of this exposition the Weird Sisters take on a dignity, a dark grandeur, and a terror-inspiring aspect which is in no way native to the witch-symbol as such. In the first place, they are clairvoyant in the sense that whatever happens outwardly among men is immediately known to them. In the thunder and lightning of a desert place they look upon the distant battle, in which Macbeth overcomes the King's enemies, and conjecture that it will be lost and won before the day ends. They do not travel to the camp near Forres where Duncan receives news of the battle, but when Macbeth is created Thane of Cawdor they seem to know it instantly. They must be aware that it is Macbeth who murders Duncan, because Hecate berates them for having trafficked with him in affairs of death without her help.[65] All the events of the drama—the murder of Banquo and the escape of Fleance, the striking down of Lady Macduff and her children, Macbeth's accumulating sins and tragic death—must, as they unfold in time, be immediately perceived by these creatures in whom the spe-

77

cies of these things are connatural. Moreover, by virtue of their spiritual substance they are acquainted with the causes of things, and, through the application of wisdom gained by long experience, are able to prognosticate future events [66] in relation to Macbeth and Banquo: Macbeth shall be king, none of woman born shall harm him, he shall never be overcome until Birnam wood shall come against him to Dunsinane; Banquo shall be no king, but he shall beget kings. The external causes upon which these predictions are based may to a certain extent be manipulated by these demonic forces; but the internal causes, *i.e.*, the forces which move the will of Macbeth to action, are imperfectly known and only indirectly subject to their influence. They cannot read his inmost thoughts—only God can do that—but from observation of facial expression and other bodily manifestations,[67] they surmise with comparative accuracy what passions drive him and what dark desires of his await their fostering. Realizing that he desires the kingdom, they prophesy that he shall be king, thus arousing his passions and inflaming his imagination to the extent that nothing is but what is not. This influence gained over him is later augmented when they cause to appear before him evil spirits, who condense the air about them into the shapes of an armed Head, a bloody Child, and a crowned Child. These demonic presences materialize to the sound of thunder and seem to speak to him with human voices, suggesting evil and urging him toward destruction with the pronouncement of half-truths. These are illusions created by demonic powers, objective appearances with a sensible content sufficient to arouse his ocular and auditory senses.

Indeed, the Weird Sisters are always illusions when they appear as such upon the stage; that is to say, their forms clothe the demonic powers which inform them.[68] This is suggested by the facility with which they materialize to human sight and disappear. King James suspects that the Devil is able to render witches invisible when he pleases,[69] but these Weird Sisters seem of their own motion to melt into thin air and vanish like a dream. Instead of disappearing with the swift movement which characterizes demonic transportation of bodies, they simply fade into nothingness. This suggests that their movements from place to place are not continuous necessarily. Though one of them plans to sail to Aleppo in a sieve, we feel that for the most part they appear in one place at one instant and at another place the next instant, or at whatever time pleases them, without being subject to the laws of time and place. I would not, however, force this point. At any rate, all their really important actions in the drama suggest that they are demons in the guise of witches.

But the witch-appearances constitute only a comparatively small part of the demonic manifestations in *Macbeth*. Many of the natural occurrences and all of the supernatural phenomena may be attributed to the activities of the metaphysical world of evil spirits. Whether visible or invisible these malignant substances insinuate themselves into the essence of the natural world and hover about the souls of men and women; they influence and in a measure direct human thought and action by means of illusions, hallucinations, and inward persuasion. For example, since they are able to manipulate nature's germens and control the winds, we may reasonably suppose that the storm which rages over Macbeth's castle and environs in Act II is no ordinary tempest caused by the regular movements of the heavenly bodies, but rather a manifestation of demonic power over the elements of nature. Indeed, natural forces seem to be partly in abeyance; o'er the one half-world nature seems dead. A strange, mephitic atmosphere hangs over and pervades the castle and adjacent country-side; an unnatural darkness, for ages the milieu of evil forces, blots out the stars and in the morning strangles the rising sun. Where Lennox lies—evidently not far distant—the night is so unruly that chimneys are blown down, lamentings and strange screams of death are heard in the air; and the firm-set earth is so sensitized by the all-pervading demonic energy that it is feverous and shakes. Macbeth senses this magnetization, and fears that the very stones will prate of his whereabouts. As the drunken Porter feels, Macbeth's castle is literally the mouth of hell through which evil spirits emerge in this darkness to cause upheavals in nature. Within the span of his seventy years the Old Man has experienced many strange and dreadful things, but they are as trifles in comparison with the occurrences of this rough night. Demonic powers are rampant in nature.

They also fill the imaginations of sleeping men with the shapes of unholy visions. Honest Banquo has kept his bosom franchised and his allegiance clear; but when his conscious mind is asleep and his will quiescent, he cannot help dreaming of the three Weird Sisters. This vision, and no doubt others like it, are so terrifying that he would not willingly sleep again, though a heavy summons to natural rest lies like lead upon him. He prays for divine protection against such dreams, recognizing apparently that their ultimate origin is demonic. At least, in his extremity he importunes precisely that order of angels which God, in his providence, has deputed to be concerned especially with the restraint and coercion of demons, namely, Powers. Says Banquo:

> Merciful Powers,
> Restrain in me the cursed thoughts that nature
> Gives way to in repose.

Moreover, immediately after Macbeth stabs the King, the spiritual world is so shaken by the evil deed that two men sleeping in an adjoining room are abused by wicked dreams. One laughs in his sleep and one cries 'Murder,' so that they wake each other. Conscious then of the demonic forces still vibrant about them, one cries 'God bless us,' and the other, 'Amen.' Such dreams may be explained upon purely natural grounds, but under the circumstances they may the more reasonably be attributed to the influence of bad angels. As Thomas Aquinas explains the matter:

Corporeal nature obeys the angel as regards local movement, so that whatever can be caused by the local movement of bodies is subject to the natural powers of the angels. Now it is manifest that imaginative apparitions are sometimes caused in us by the local movements of animal spirits and humours. Hence Aristotle says, when assigning a cause of visions in dreams, that 'when an animal sleeps, the blood descends in abundance to the sensitive principle, and movements descend with it,' that is, the impressions left from the movements of sensible things, which movements are preserved in the animal spirits, 'and move the sensitive principle'; so that a certain appearance ensues, as if the sensitive principle were being changed by external objects themselves. Indeed, the commotion of the spirits and humours may be so great that such appearances may even occur to those who are awake, as is seen in mad people, and the like. So as this happens by a natural disturbance of the humours, and sometimes also by the will of man who voluntarily imagines what he previously experienced, so also the same may be done by the power of a good or a bad angel, sometimes with alienation from bodily senses, sometimes without such alienation (I. 111. 3. c.).

This exposition also offers a basis for judgment concerning the nature of Macbeth's vision of a bloody dagger, which seems to swim in the air and marshal him to the murder of Duncan. It may be either an illusion or an hallucination, but more likely the latter. If it is an illusion, the source of it is demonic; for, says James, 'the deuil may forme what kinde of impressiones he pleases in the aire.' If the air-drawn dagger is an hallucination,[70] the cause of it may be either simple or complex. Whatever the complication may be, it is in that case a false creation of the mind proceeding immediately from the local movements of humours in the heat-oppressed brain of Macbeth. It is in appearance just such a dagger as he is to use presently. If anyone likes to have it so, the tense state of Macbeth's mind in this situation accounts sufficiently and fully for the phenomenon, and there is psychological evidence from Aristotle to Shakespeare in support of this interpretation. But, as most writers on hallucinations in the Middle Ages and in the Renaissance also agree, it is just these disordered bodily humours that the devil and his angels find to be the best media through which they may impose upon man's senses, deceive his imagination, becloud his reason, and so lead him to his destruction.[71] As Nashe says:

So the Devill when with any other sickness or malladie the faculties of our reason are enfeebled and distempered, will be most busie to disturbe us and torment us. . . . Children, fooles, sicke-men, or mad-men hee is most familiar with . . . and to whom he boldly revealeth the whole astonishing treasurie of his wonders.[72]

We may safely conclude, then, that Macbeth's vision of a dagger is an hallucination caused immediately, indeed, by disturbed bodily humours and spirits but ultimately by demonic powers, who have so controlled and manipulated these bodily forces as to produce the effect they desire. And a like explanation may be offered of the mysterious voice which Macbeth seems to hear after the murder, crying exultantly to all the house, 'Sleep no more! Macbeth does murder sleep.' [73]

Entrance of Banquo's ghost precipitates a most intricate problem. What exactly is the nature of this particular ghost? Any adequate answer to this question involves consideration of enlightened opinion regarding ghosts in Shakespeare's time. Realists of the age would say that Banquo's ghost is nothing more than an hallucination, a creature of Macbeth's imagination, produced by the perturbation of humours through fear; [74] others with a sensitiveness to the occult would hold, however, that the hallucination so produced is ultimately to be attributed to the activities of demonic powers, as in the case of the dagger and the voice. Both Protestants and Catholics would agree that it is possible for a human being to imagine seeing a ghost under these circumstances. But Professor Stoll's arguments against hallucination as an explanation of Banquo's ghost are, it seems to me, unanswerable.[75] Further, this particular ghost can be considered, in the light of Catholic faith from Aquinas to Le Loyer, as either the actual spirit of Banquo returned from Purgatory to take revenge upon the murderer, or as an illusion in his likeness created out of air by the devil or his angels.[76] Protestants, on the other hand, would say that it cannot be the specter of Banquo at all; barring hallucination, it must be in reality the Devil in an illusory form resembling Banquo's, or that same evil spirit animating (though not vitalizing) Banquo's dead body.[77] It must be observed that even the Catholics, though they affirm the possibility of the soul's return from Purgatory, are quick to admit that there is nothing in nature to account for it; such apparitions are miracles wrought by the will of God and do not often occur.[78] Thus in Shakespeare's time all parties (except realists) seem to be convinced that in the great majority of instances ghost appearances are in reality illusions created by good or bad angels. Even when the ghost seems gentle, one cannot be sure that a good angel is responsible for it; for demons have the power of assuming shapes which might ordinarily be attributed to the good angels.[79] We may logically conclude, then, that Banquo's ghost is an infernal illusion, created out of air by demonic forces and presented to Macbeth's sight at the banquet in order that the murderer may be confused and utterly confounded. The second appearance of Banquo's ghost, together with the show of eight kings (IV, i, 112), is undoubtedly the result of demonic machinations. Having persuaded and otherwise incited Macbeth to sin and crime, the Devil and his angels now employ illusions which lead to his betrayal and final destruction.

And finally, certain aspects of Lady Macbeth's experience indicate that she is possessed of demons. At least, in preparation for the coming of Duncan under her battlements, she calls upon precisely those metaphysical forces which have seemed to crown Macbeth. The murdering ministers whom she invokes for aid are described as being sightless substances, *i.e.*, not evil thoughts and 'grim imaginings' but objective substantial forms, invisible bad angels, to whose activities may be attributed all the unnatural occurrences of nature. Whatever in the phenomenal world becomes beautiful in the exercise of its normal function is to them foul, and *vice versa;* they wait upon nature's mischief. She recognizes that they infest the filthy atmosphere of this world and the blackness of the lower regions; therefore she welcomes a night palled in the dunnest smoke of hell, so dense that not even heaven may pierce the blanket of the dark and behold her projected deed. Her prayer is apparently answered; with the coming of night her castle is, as we have seen, shrouded in just such a blackness as she desires. She knows also that these spiritual substances study eagerly the effects of mental activities upon the human body, waiting patiently for evidences of evil thought which will permit them entrance past the barriers of the human will into the body to possess it. They tend on mortal thoughts. For, says Cassian: 'It is clear that unclean spirits cannot make their way into those bodies they are going to seize upon, in any other way than by first taking possession of their minds and thoughts.' [80] Thus instead of guarding the workings of her mind against the assaults of wicked angels, Lady Macbeth deliberately wills that they subtly invade her body and so control it that the natural inclinations of the spirit toward goodness and compassion may be completely extirpated. Says she:

Come you spirits,
That tend on mortal thoughts, unsex me here,
And fill me from the crown to the toe, top-full
Of direst cruelty; make thick my blood,
Stop up th'access and passage to remorse,
That no compunctious visitings of nature
Shake my fell purpose, nor keep peace between
Th'effect and it. Come to my woman's breasts
And take my milk for gall, you murth'ring ministers,
Wherever, in your sightless substances,
You wait on nature's mischief (I, v, 45–55).

And without doubt these ministers of evil do actually take possession of her body even in accordance with her desire. As Mrs. Siddons remarks: 'Having

87

impiously delivered herself up to the excitements of hell, the pitifulness of heaven itself is withdrawn from her, and she is abandoned to the guidance of the demons whom she has invoked.' [81]

Possession of Lady Macbeth's body enables these forces of evil to control her spirit. As Cassian says: 'It is a fact that those men are more grievously and severely troubled who, while they seem to be very little affected by them in the body, are yet possessed in spirit in a far worse way, as they are entangled in their sins.' [82] We must not imagine that this possession of spirit is accomplished by the infusion of the demonic substance in such a way that it actually penetrates the substance of the soul—only the spirit of God may be fused in this manner with the spirit of man. Rather the unclean spirits overwhelm the intellectual nature of man only when they are permitted to seize upon those members in which the vitality of the soul resides.[83] This is what happens to Lady Macbeth. The forces which take possession of her body do unsex her and fill her from crown to toe, top-full of direst cruelty; they thicken her blood and so stop up the passage to remorse. She becomes, for the most part, the fiend-like queen in thought and action. 'Not a single sentiment of repentance is betrayed . . . in the course of her whole criminal career. Nothing like remorse can be discovered from her expressions. In truth, the only feeling of *human* nature which she, at any time, exhibits, and that alone

88

which redeems her from being an incarnate fiend, is the tender remembrance of her father, which prevented her plunging the poniard into the body of her sleeping sovereign, as she quitted her chamber purposely to do.' [84] Though this compunctious visiting of nature does not shake her ultimate purpose of having the king murdered, still it indicates that demonic powers have not gained absolute control over her soul; no human being can become completely evil.[85]

What happens to Lady Macbeth in the course of Act IV is not immediately clear. Apparently there is a steady deterioration of her demon-possessed body until, at the beginning of Act V, the organs of her spirit are impaired to the point of imminent dissolution. Such a great perturbation of nature has seized upon her that she walks night after night in slumbery agitation, with eyes wide open but with the senses shut. There appears a definite cleavage in her personality. Her will, which in conscious moments guards against any revelation of her guilty experiences, is submerged; and her infected mind is forced to discharge its secrets in the presence of alien ears. Her symptoms in these circumstances resemble those of the ordinary somnambulist,[86] but the violence of her reactions indicates that her state is what may be called 'somnambuliform possession' or 'demoniacal somnambulism.' As Professor Oesterreich says:

Typical possession is . . . distinguished from ordinary somnambulistic states by its intense motor and emotional excitement, so much so that we might hesitate to take it for a form of somnambulism but for the fact that possession is so nearly related to the ordinary form of these states that it is impossible to avoid classing them together.[87]

The most outstanding characteristic of this demoniacal somnambulism, which in the course of history has been more common than any other form of possession, is that the normal individuality disappears and seems to be replaced by a second personality, which speaks through the patient's mouth. This strange individuality always confesses wrong-doing, and sometimes relates a sort of life-history consisting frequently of the patient's reminiscences or memories.[88] Now the physician to Lady Macbeth recognizes these symptoms in his patient.[89] Sometimes, to be sure, he has known those who have walked in their sleep who have died holily in their beds. But this disease is beyond his practice; this heart sorely charged with perilous stuff needs the divine more than the physician. The demonic substances she welcomed into her body now employ her bodily functions to disclose her criminal experiences. As Professor Tolman well says: 'In this scene . . . it is the invisible world of moral reality which is made strangely manifest before our eyes. Lady Macbeth would not reveal those guilty secrets for all the wealth of all the world. . . . Her feet, her hands,

90

her lips, conspire against her. In the presence of the awful, unseen Power that controls her poor, divided self, we hush the breath and bow the head.' [90]

Shakespeare's age would undoubtedly have pronounced Lady Macbeth's sleep-walking an instance of demoniacal somnambulism. Practically everybody, so far as may be determined, accepted demonic possession as an established fact. The New Testament affirmed it; the Church Fathers had elaborated and illustrated it; the Catholic Church made of it a firm article of faith and proceeded to exorcise demons by means of recognized rituals involving holy-water and cross, bell, book, and candle; and Protestants could not consistently deny it, or if some of them did, peremptory experience forced them to take a doubtful refuge in the conception of obsession, which produced the effects of possession.[91] Martin Luther certainly considered 'all mental affections as possession, and suicide as one of their consequences.' In these circumstances he cannot, of course, have rejected the interpretation of true states of possession as such; he rather personally undertook exorcisms of the possessed (1545) . . . with 'prayer and contempt.' [92] He and other Protestants, however, opposed the Papist doctrine of exorcism on the grounds that it concentrates too much power in the hands of man; God's servants should rather fast and pray without ceasing until God hears their prayer.[93] King James prepared for Philomathes a list of infallible symptoms, by which one might distinguish diabolical possession from ordinary insanity.[94] Physicians were likely to attribute diseases they did not understand to the activities of devils.[95] It does not seem necessary to revive here the bitter controversy, which shook Elizabethan England, regarding the efficacy of Popish exorcism of unclean spirits.[96] But vehement charges of fraud and countercharges of blasphemy, theological chop-logic and hair-splitting, serve to emphasize the importance of demonic possession for the Elizabethan mind.[97] Fortunately Shakespeare has spared us, in the case of Lady Macbeth, a representation of the more disgusting physical symptoms of the diabolically possessed, such as astounding contortions of the body and fantastic creations of the delirious mind.[98] He merely suggests these horrors in the report of the Doctor that the Lady is troubled with thick-coming fancies and in the expressed opinion of some that she took her own life by self and violent hands. He is interested primarily in presenting not so much the physical as the spiritual disintegration of this soul-weary creature possessed of devils.

In this manner, it seems to me, Shakespeare has informed *Macbeth* with the Christian conception of a metaphysical world of objective evil. The whole drama is saturated with the malignant presences of demonic forces; they animate nature and ensnare human souls by means of diabolical persuasion, by hallucination, infernal illusion, and possession. They are, in the strictest sense, one element in that Fate which God in his providence has ordained to rule over the bodies and, it is possible, over the spirits of men. And the essence of this whole metaphysical world of evil intelligences is distilled by Shakespeare's imagination and concentrated in those marvellous dramatic symbols, the Weird Sisters. The story of evil in *Macbeth,* however, is not with these considerations complete. We have scarcely touched upon that subjective evil, whose origin lies somewhere in the perverted will of man. Before a basis for full interpretation of the drama can be established, therefore, it will be necessary to consider the nature of Macbeth as man and individual, the quality of his moral responsibilities and derelictions, and to trace the pattern of his relationship to such an objective world of evil as we have described.

*Behold, all souls are mine;*
*As the soul of the father,*
*So also the soul of the son is mine:*
*The soul that sinneth, it shall die.*

EZEKIEL

# CHAPTER IV

## MACBETH'S CHANGING CHARACTER *

I

SHAKESPEARE's *Macbeth* may be regarded as a vivid study in the ravages of external and internal evil. We have already examined elsewhere [1] the conceptions of external evil involved in the dramatic action and have found them thoroughly Christian and mediaeval. The whole drama is discovered to be saturated with the malignant presences of demons or fallen angels; they animate nature and ensnare human souls by means of diabolical persuasion, by hallucination, infernal illusions, and possession. This objective world of evil may be thought of as one term in a set of relationships which constitute the philosophical pattern of the tragedy. Another term is Macbeth himself. It is now the general purpose of this present chapter, therefore, to examine that subjective evil whose origin lies somewhere in the misdirected or perverted will of Macbeth, to consider his nature as man and individual, to discover the rationale of his changing or deteriorating character,

* This chapter appeared first in *JEGPh.*, XXXIV (1935), 311 ff.

and to trace the pattern of his relationships to the objective world of evil about him.

It would be impossible, one may suppose, to pluck out the heart of Macbeth's mystery. In attempted reconstructions of his character, nevertheless, many 'notes' have been struck and a bewildering variety of 'keys' have been fashioned. One critic, for example, finds that the 'note, as it may be called, of Macbeth is the weakness of a bold mind, a vigorous body,'[2] and one actor 'sees nothing great in him beyond the royalty of muscle and that courage which comes of strong and copious circulation.'[3] Another actor conceives of him as a 'villain cold-blooded, selfish, remorseless, with a true villain's nerve and callousness when braced to evil work and the physical heroism of those who are born to kill.'[4] He has, on the other hand, been called 'the perfect type of the man of action, so far as such perfection is possible where there has been no culture of the life within'; his is the 'practical nature' which wants 'self-discipline' and so 'fails in self-conflict.'[5] He is further represented as being 'a most wonderful example of the excited intellect running away, the will being powerless to stop it'; his 'double character' is 'half-way between the mere man of thought, like Hamlet, and the ideal man of action, like Othello.'[6] A 'mental physiologist, to whom nerve rather than conscience, the function of the brain rather than the power of will, is the object of study,' pronounces him

98

'a man of sanguine nervous temperament, of large capacity and ready susceptibility . . . a man of nervous instability,' whose high energy and courage are nothing more than 'qualities of nerve force.' [7] Schücking diagnoses his case as pathological; this 'weak man' is said to be the 'victim of his nerves. No doubt of their diseased condition can arise when we find him suffering from unmistakable hallucinations of the visual and auditory organs.' [8] For Adams, 'Macbeth's character is simple: the two dominant forces that control his actions are ambition and conscience. He is so ambitious that he is potentially capable of the worst crime. Yet from crime he is held back by the second great force in his nature, namely, conscience. When the two forces struggle within him for mastery, conscience is able to dominate . . . because it holds a whip hand over him in the form of horrid images that shake him with fear.' [9] Stoll discovers in him a contrast 'between the man and his conscience. . . . And . . . the conscience is of that external sort—the voice of a better nature within him, not of the character's own. . . . He is psychologically . . . reduced to the lowest terms, to the murderer and his conscience; and a conscience not, after its wont, clad in the man's own desires or appetites, and sneakingly lending approval, but rising up in its stark reality to bar the way.' [10] Campbell will have it that he is brought to a tragic end through action of 'the complementary pair of passions of rash courage and fear.' [11] Croce wishes the evil in him to be called *greatness* and the good which opposes it to be considered of a 'lofty quality, gentle and serene, planted in the heart of Macbeth and called by the name of loyalty, duty, justice, respect for the being of others, human piety.' [12] Bradley speaks of him as a 'bold ambitious man of action . . . a great warrior, somewhat masterful, rough, and abrupt,' who is endowed with 'the imagination of a poet—an imagination on the one hand extremely sensitive to impressions of a certain kind, and, on the other, productive of violent disturbance both of mind and body.' [13] And Knight is of the opinion that 'Macbeth, like the whole universe of this play, is paralysed, mesmerized, as though in a dream. This is not merely "ambition"—it is fear, a nameless fear which yet fixes itself to a horrid image. He is helpless as a man in a nightmare: and this helplessness is integral to the conception—the will-concept is absent.' [14]

There is probably much virtue in these estimates, but no one of them nor a composite of all can successfully delimit the bounds of Macbeth's character. For Macbeth is a quick character-creation, an artistic reflection of life after the best Shakespeare manner; consequently, his qualities are innumerable and the motives which actuate him are abundant and inextricable. As a living personality acting in his own world, Macbeth must be abstruse, complex, and

**100**

highly problematic. And to attempt confining him within the limits of a scholarly or critical theory is to follow the methods of scientists who would reduce the infinite contingencies of life and nature to a formula. No formula can be equivalent to the full Macbeth, and no 'key' quite unlocks his intricate personality. Still, reactions to his character by persons within and without the play must always be as varied as those of different personalities to a given character in real life. In their estimates of him Lady Macbeth no more agrees with Macduff than, say, Stoll with Schücking. All can agree, however, that, descriptively speaking, he is in some sense a man of action, he possesses some kind of imagination, he displays a sort of courage, he is at times hounded apparently by fears, upon occasion his nerves are not normally quiet, and that he suffers from what has the appearance of conscience. He himself thinks that ambition is one of the most powerful motives to action; he and others surmise that in some sense a profound alteration of something within him takes place during the progress of the action. But no accumulation of descriptive phrases can denote Macbeth truly, and no multiplication of personal reactions to his character can sound him from his lowest note to the top of his compass. The wide variety of critical estimates, however, attests his tremendous vitality as an artistic creation.

A more effective procedure, it seems to me, might

be to attempt even an approximate understanding of Shakespeare's Macbeth. This must be more difficult than mere personal reaction for several reasons. We may suppose, in the first place, that Shakespeare like all other artists never quite succeeds in expressing adequately in objective form his original conception. The Macbeth presented in this poetic drama is an organic construction in the phenomenal world in which the poet attempts to fix for himself and for us such aspects of his vision as will suggest to us the whole of his intuitive experience. Perfect communication is presumably not attained, however, because his medium is only partially tractable. But, in the second place, granting that the externalization of his character-conception is adequate, difficulties in the way of our understanding it are almost insurmountable. For Macbeth's character is an artistic fact produced in situations and under circumstances quite at variance with those familiar to us. The content of Shakespeare's conception represents a fusion of many elements foreign in a measure to our modern experience. That is to say, Macbeth is a product of the Italian Renaissance and of the traditions which stretch back of it. If we are to understand him at all, therefore, we must reproduce historically and as fully as possible the stimuli which urged Shakespeare to create him. In this way, the proper psychological conditions having been reintegrated in us, we may enable Macbeth's character to act upon us ap-

102

proximately as it acted upon Shakespeare. Even so, because all the possible stimuli are not recoverable, we must ultimately and inevitably content ourselves with a Macbeth only more or less resembling that character which the dramatist has attempted to present in the play. Now this present study cannot undertake to collect and focus upon Macbeth's personality anything like all the pertinent facts among which it arose nor to concern itself greatly with any mechanical succession of 'influences.' It attempts to furnish merely a partial basis for interpretation by recreating a background of philosophical principles and traditions—without emphasizing definite lines of reference—which Shakespeare more or less unconsciously assimilated and allowed to modify his conception of Macbeth's character. The traditions in question are those of scholastic philosophy, which the Renaissance inherits from the Middle Ages, and the principles involve definite concepts of human free-will and freedom of choice, the essence of man as moral being together with the origin, nature, and effect of internal evil or sin, the function of conscience, and the physics of change in character.

## II

Let us make some tentative observations regarding Macbeth. We have in him, let us say, a man of colossal proportions who seems to be exercising an essentially noble nature in a struggle for happiness. In the beginning of the drama he is apparently provided with a definite disposition and with certain inclinations (no doubt the result in part of habitual thought and action). His will seems to be entirely untrammeled and his liberty of free choice absolute. His decision to commit regicide, however, is influenced in some way by an inordinate passion, by reason impaired through disordered imagination, by his wife, and by such evil forces as are symbolized in the Weird Sisters. After the first crime, however, one cannot help observing that a change has taken place in the man. This must not be taken to mean that as a dramatic character he is not consistently drawn; artistically speaking, Macbeth is always himself. Nor are we to suppose that his development during the progress of the play is merely a further revelation regarding the man whom we know but imperfectly upon first acquaintance. Nor does the change in him represent merely a shift in point of view or in attitude. It is rather a profound alteration in the state of his personality, an astounding dislocation of the very center of being, which fixes itself immediately in a habit inclining to further crime. This change is progressive: while sin plucks on sin, the good in him seems to diminish, leaving his nature finally an almost completely barren waste of evil. But he is never quite completely evil. His knowledge of right and wrong flowers into the act of conscience, which witnesses through spiritual and mental suffering to the alteration in him. Since the good in him can never be quite destroyed, we experience even at the end a sort of admiration for the ultimate dignity of the human spirit.

In the meantime, throughout the play his will continues to function in what seem to be acts of free choice. One feels, however, that, in proportion as the good in him diminishes, his liberty of free choice is determined more and more by evil inclination and that he cannot choose the better course. Hence we speak of destiny or fate, as if it were some external force or moral order, compelling him against his will to certain destruction. Whether this force which we sense is intrinsic or extrinsic, whether it is absolute or limited, is not immediately clear. At any rate, accompanying the phenomenon of change in being, we have a passage from a strict indeterminism to an apparent determinism. In short, Macbeth's spiritual experience is a representation on the stage of the traditional Christian conception of a human soul on its way to the Devil. Let us observe its progress in the light of traditional conceptions developed and transmitted by those teachers of the Renaissance, the scholastic philosophers.

Scholastic philosophy is a pluralistic philosophy which emphasizes the ultimate importance of the inviolable individual. Its metaphysics deals with the infinite variety of changing things, its physics and moral philosophy with the mysterious complexity, in potency and act, of the individual human personality. Consequently, the human being is invested with a sublime dignity, and his actions, cosmic in importance, are directed to ineffable ends. Unlike other creatures, he is endowed with a rational soul having two god-like powers: namely, intellect or understanding, with which he discovers truth, and will, with which he desires good. As to the relative superiority of these two powers, the scholastics are divided, some giving the supremacy to intellect and its function, reason, others to will and its function, liberty of free choice. But in either case man is a reasonable being, who has been given the freedom to work out his own destiny according to his nature.[15]

In any adequate system of moral philosophy this responsibility placed upon man is dependent upon the psychological conception of freedom, that is, freedom of the will to choose among a variety of motives. Already Plato affirms man's freedom of choice and moral responsibility in addition to the ethical conception of Socrates that only the wise man is free.[16] Aristotle postulates a psychological freedom of choice which under certain circumstances conditions ethical responsibility, but he does not speculate upon the matter of motivation and the compelling causes of choice.[17] It is that grand old Briton, Pelagius, who first in the Christian tradition emphasizes the absolute freedom of the human will

106

and the essential nobility of human nature as the central principles of his system. While Augustine insists upon natural depravity of the human will after the Fall until it is regenerated by grace,[18] Pelagius teaches that every man is born sinless as Adam and entirely competent of himself to all good through the exercise of freedom of choice. For him this 'freedom is the supreme good, the honor and glory of man, the *bonum naturae*, which cannot be lost.'[19] Says he:

Now we have implanted in us by God a capacity for either good or evil. It resembles, as I may say, a fruitful and fecund root which yields and produces diversely according to the will of man, and which is capable, at the planter's own choice, of either shedding a beautiful bloom of virtues, or of bristling with the thorny thickets of vice.[20]

Pelagius ignores the power of habit upon the liberty of free choice—and in this his conception is very limited—but he cannot be given too much credit for having formulated this idea of the essential nobility of the human spirit and this conception of freedom of the will.

Thanks partly to opposition and partly to their affinity with the Western mind, his principles have survived in some form to the present day; indeed, as Schaff remarks, 'all rationalists are Pelagian in their anthropology.'[21] But his most immediate successors in mediaeval philosophy are the scholastics, particularly that group functioning in the Franciscan tradition. For example, we find Alexander of

Hales affirming the principle of original righteous-
ness and superadded grace; Bonaventura, while ob-
sessed primarily with the idea of God, has time to
assert that man has power to do 'that which is in
himself.' [22] John Pecham first maintains the primacy
of will over intellect, observing that 'voluntas seu
liberum arbitrium . . . movetur a se.' [23] Richard of
Middleton agrees that, though the act of understanding is necessary in free choice, the will has the ability to move itself in choosing its ends.[24] And Duns
Scotus, representing the culmination of this liberal
movement, conceives of every act of the will as being absolutely spontaneous and free; one of the conditions, to be sure, upon which it acts is the representation of the good and reasonable by the intellect,
but the will is always able to choose whatever course
it desires. He is quick to state, however, that the
elicited act of the will is not capricious but a moti-
vated and reasoned act.[25] This indeterminism or vol-
untarism of the Franciscan school does not differ
greatly from the so-called determinism of Thomas
Aquinas, for whom the voluntary act is intrinsically
determined by the intellectual presentation of the
*complete* good.[26] Thus the greatest thinkers of both
schools agree that it is the very nature of the human
will to desire good, whether impelled or merely inclined by the reasonable representation of it. This
'true and ultimate human good must be that which
satisfies specifically human aspirations, and answers

108

to the most elevated tendencies, the intellect and will.' [27] And wherever original sin is recognized at all, it is reduced to a mere innocuous inclination of the passions to inordinateness.[28] For the scholastics, then, freedom combines power of choice with action in accordance with the highest and most essential elements in man's nature; and since acts of free choice are directed toward a known end, volition must in a measure be identified with character.[29] Here we have, surely, an ample background for the Renaissance appreciation of the individual and for that independence of spirit which affirms that man is the arbiter of his own fortunes.[30]

III

Now by what processes does this essentially noble creature, whose will by nature desires the good or reasonable, come deliberately to choose evil? To answer this vital question we must determine the relationship between the intellect and reason, on the one hand, and will and free-will, on the other. As Thomas Aquinas explains it, the intellect or understanding is that power of the rational soul by which one apprehends an intelligible truth or simply knows first principles; the reason is that same power in the act of comparing and judging conclusions and of progressing to new knowledge (I. 79. 1–8).[31] The will is that power of the soul which desires 'ultimate ends, good and happiness'; free-will is that same power in the act of 'choosing appropriate means to those ends' (I. 83. 4). Free-will is, therefore, a faculty of both will and reason, since both powers are involved in any act of free choice (I. 83. 3, 4). No power can move the human will directly except the *necessity of end,* which is that movement toward the good or apparent good which comes by nature from God.[32] All extrinsic coercion, or the *necessity of coercion* by agents, is altogether abhorrent to the very nature of the will (I. 82. 1. c.). Intrinsically, however, it may be moved indirectly, though never necessitated, in two ways: First, the will, which is naturally inclined to follow the judgments of reason, is moved to error in its acts of free choice when reason's knowledge of the ultimate good is defective or when its judgment regarding the present good is perverted by a 'vehement and inordinate apprehension of the imagination and judgment of the estimative power,' which follow the passions of the sensitive appetite (I–II. 77. 1). And secondly, the passions of the sensitive appetite tend to distract the will from its normal functions (I–II. 77. 2). Thus neither human being nor Devil has any power to coerce or directly compel the free-will of man; but they may exert a powerfully impelling or persuasive influence by distracting the will or by working through the passions, which move the inordinate imagination to cloud the

110

reason and so lead the will to an act of sin (I–II. 75. 3).

We have observed elsewhere [33] that Christian philosophy solves the problem of the duality of good and evil by assuming that God originally provided human souls with a freedom similar to his own and that subjective evil or sin resulted from the opposition of the creature's will to the divine will. This original sin of Adam still finds expression in human nature as a sort of habit. 'For,' says Thomas, 'it is an inordinate disposition, arising from the destruction of the harmony which was essential to original justice' (I–II. 82. 1). It is precisely this inordinate disposition, coupled with an expression of self-will, which is responsible for individual sin in the human heart. Thomas Aquinas explains it this way: the direct cause of sin is the 'adherence to a mutable good,' and every sinful act proceeds from an inordinate desire for some temporal good (I–II. 75. 1); and that one desires a temporal good inordinately is due to the fact that 'he loves himself inordinately.' Thus love of self is the fundamental cause of sin (I–II. 77. 4). Now certain actions are called human or moral or good inasmuch as they proceed from reason; evil implies 'privation of good, and it acts always in virtue of deficient goodness' (I–II. 18. 1, 5).[34] The self-lover, therefore, who loves more the lesser good, may deliberately choose spiritual evil and may even come to sin through

111

'certain malice' (I–II. 78. 2). But, it must be observed, 'he cannot intend evil for its own sake, though he may intend it for the sake of avoiding another evil or obtaining another good' (I–II. 78. 1). Thus the Christian conception of evil combines the negative element of departure from God, the absence of good, with a positive element involving the rebellion of the perverted finite will against the mandates of the infinite will.

IV

Now this, it seems to me, might well serve as a basis for an exact analysis of Macbeth's inner state and fundamental experiences in the first act of the drama. He is presented as a mature man of definitely established character, successful in certain fields of activity and enjoying an enviable reputation. We must not conclude, therefore, that all his volitions and actions are predictable; Macbeth's character, like any other man's at a given moment, is what is being made out of potentialities plus environment, and no one, not even Macbeth himself, can know all his potentialities. It is clear, however, that he is first revealed as a man of inordinate self-love whose actions are discovered to be—and no doubt have been for a long time—determined mainly by an inordinate desire for some temporal or mutable good. He is capable of conceiving of ultimate and lofty ends; he knows what it is to be actively loyal to king and country, to accept duty, to promote justice, amity, and piety. But he is inclined to center his attention upon the means to those ends with the primary purpose, not of attaining ultimate good, but of flattering his inordinate love of self. Or the inordinateness of his desire for some temporal good may express itself in an unwillingness or incapacity to control properly the means to that end. Or his desire for a temporal good may be so overwhelming that he is willing to resort to improper means of attaining it, provided always that the employment of such means does not afflict his self-love with loss of satisfactions which attainment of the end cannot counterpoise.

That is to say, Macbeth is actuated in his conduct mainly by an inordinate desire for worldly honors; his delight lies primarily in buying golden opinions from all sorts of people. But we must not, therefore, deny him an entirely human complexity of motives. For example, his fighting in Duncan's service is magnificent and courageous, and his evident joy in it is traceable in part to the natural pleasure which accompanies the explosive expenditure of prodigious physical energy and the euphoria which follows. He also rejoices no doubt in the success which crowns his efforts in battle—and so on. He may even conceive of the proper motive which should energize back of his great deed:

> The service and the loyalty I owe,
> In doing it, pays itself.

113

But while he destroys the king's enemies, such motives work but dimly at best and are obscured in his consciousness by more vigorous urges. In the main, as we have said, his nature violently demands rewards: he fights valiantly in order that he may be reported in such terms as 'valour's minion' and 'Bellona's bridegroom'; he values success because it brings spectacular fame and new titles and royal favor heaped upon him in public. Now so long as these mutable goods are at all commensurate with his inordinate desires—and such is the case, up until he covets the kingship—Macbeth remains an honorable gentleman. He is not a criminal; he has no criminal tendencies. But once permit his self-love to demand a satisfaction which cannot be honorably attained, and he is likely to grasp any dishonorable means to that end which may be safely employed. In other words, Macbeth has much of *natural* good in him unimpaired; environment has conspired with his nature to make him upright in all his dealings with those about him. But *moral* goodness in him is undeveloped and indeed still rudimentary, for his voluntary acts are scarcely brought into harmony with ultimate ends.[35]

Lady Macbeth evidently understands thoroughly this aspect of his nature. The natural good in him—in this case expressing itself as 'an instinctive tendency to shrink from what is in any way unnatural'[36] —she calls 'the milk of human kindness.' This is what causes in him an entirely human revulsion of feeling

114

against actions not in harmony with man's nature;
and this, she fears, is what may prevent his catching
the *nearest* way to his greatest desire; the kingship.
Heretofore, time and the hour have run through Macbeth's roughest day; all his honors have come to him
in the natural sequence of worthy deeds followed by
adequate recompense. Thus his highest accomplish-
ments may be said to have been executed holily, and
he can rejoice in the universal approval of the means
employed. Lady Macbeth recognizes that nothing less
than such a complete gratification of his self-love can
discharge fully the demands of his nature. She fears,
therefore, that contemplation of the ills which should
accompany regicide—such as discovery, loss of reputation, universal condemnation of the horrid deed—
may cause him to forego any attempt upon the desired end. Says she:

>  . . . yet I do fear thy nature;
> It is too full o' the milk of human kindness
> To catch the nearest way. Thou wouldst be great;
> Art not without ambition, but without
> The illness should attend it. What thou wouldst highly,
> Thou wouldst holily; wouldst not play false,
> And yet wouldst wrongly win (I, v, 17 ff.).

And the events which follow indicate that her estimate of his character is fundamentally correct.

Under the stress of temptation these developments
of potentialities in Macbeth's nature are clearly re-

vealed. Before the tragedy opens his inordinate desires have aimed at the crown of Scotland, and he has contemplated as a swift means of attaining it the murder of Duncan. Nothing came of it, however, because neither time nor place did then adhere. But as he returns from victorious battle, puffed up with self-love which demands ever-increasing recognition of his greatness, the demonic forces of evil—symbolized by the Weird Sisters—suggest to his inordinate imagination the splendid prospect of attaining now the greatest mutable good he has ever desired. These demons in the guise of witches cannot read his inmost thoughts, but from observation of facial expression and other bodily manifestations they surmise with comparative accuracy what passions drive him and what dark desires await their fostering. Realizing that he wishes the kingdom, they prophesy that he shall be king. They cannot thus compel his will to evil; but they do arouse his passions and stir up a vehement and inordinate apprehension of the imagination, which so perverts the judgment of reason that it leads his will toward choosing means to the desired temporal good. Indeed his imagination and passions are so vivid under this evil impulse from without that 'nothing is but what is not'; and his reason is so impeded that he judges, 'These solicitings cannot be evil, cannot be good.' Still, he is provided with so much natural good that he is able to control the apprehensions of his inordinate imagination and de-

cides to take no step involving crime. His autonomous
decision not to commit murder, however, is not in any
sense based upon moral grounds. No doubt he normally shrinks from the unnaturalness of regicide;
but he so far ignores ultimate ends that, if he could
perform the deed and escape its consequences here
upon this bank and shoal of time, he'ld jump the life
to come. Without denying him still a complexity of
motives—as kinsman and subject he may possibly
experience some slight shade of unmixed loyalty to
the King under his roof—we may even say that the
consequences which he fears are not at all inward and
spiritual. It is to be doubted whether he has ever so
far considered the possible effects of crime and evil
upon the human soul—his later discovery of horrible
ravages produced by evil in his own spirit constitutes
part of the tragedy. He is mainly concerned, as we
might expect, with consequences involving the loss of
mutable goods which he already possesses and values
highly: the King has honored him much of late, he has
elicited favorable opinions from all sorts of people,
and he would enjoy these newest rewards now instead
of risking them in an attempt to gain a greater temporal good. He must inevitably lose these satisfactions, he feels, because of the enormity of the crime
contemplated. Observe: condemnation pronounced by
his social order must be extraordinarily severe when
the murder is committed by a kinsman and host upon
a guest and king; and Duncan's very virtues must so

plead against the deep damnation of his taking off that pity shall blow the deed in every eye. He will proceed no further in this business—unless—

At this critical juncture, Lady Macbeth exerts her influence upon his will through the only channels possible and moves it indirectly. She is aware that an appeal to his undeveloped moral sense would be useless; she never attempts to direct his reason toward the formation of an ethical judgment upon the proposed murder. Indeed, her purposes include the prevention of such a judgment. Knowing that movements of the sensitive appetite have power to distract the will or to so work upon the imagination that reason is impeded, she moves swiftly to strike at Macbeth's will and reason through his passions. He cannot have helped marking that his masculine fearlessness and physical courage in action are the main stimuli in the production of those honors which most comfort his self-love. Indeed his personal conception of self is based upon the consciousness of his unimpeachable bravery; he dares do all that may become a man. And it is precisely this established foundation of his self-esteem that Lady Macbeth assaults. She charges him with unmasculine weakness and contemptible cowardice; his act and valor lag behind his desire; the hope even wherein he dressed himself is green and pale in the presence of necessary action; he would forego the supreme ornament of life because he lacks the sustained purpose to grasp it; he must henceforth

118

live a coward in his own esteem. She, a frail woman, would under similar circumstances display more masculine vigor than he. This affront to his manhood by the woman he loves is more than he can stand. His will is fearfully distracted by the inordinate passions which she arouses in him and is thus led to a provisional approval of the deed. But he must still face the possibility of failure and, in consequence, the loss of all those goods which he so highly prizes. And here she unfolds before his excited imagination a plan which should insure the act's being performed in absolute safety. His reason, impeded by this apprehension of the imagination, leads his will to complete acquiescence. He is settled, and bends up each corporal agent to this terrible feat. And Duncan is murdered. Thus a naturally good man, exercising within the limitations of his character the liberty of free choice, comes by perfectly normal processes to the commission of his first crime.

## V

Now the scholastics affirm that one evil act, *i.e.*, a sin, may be the efficient, material, and final cause of other sins. 'For,' says Thomas, 'when man through one sinful act loses honor, charity, or shame, or anything else that withdraws him from evil, he thereby falls into another sin, the first being the accidental cause of the second.' Or he may commit one sin for the sake of another which is his end. Or since actions cause dispositions and habits in the will inclining to like actions, 'a man is disposed by one sinful act to commit more readily another like act' (I–II. 75. 4). All these causes are active in producing the train of crimes and sins following upon Macbeth's first crime. The murder of the King disposes him to commit more easily the second murder, and the second, the third; it also removes honor, charity, and shame, so that he finally becomes, a Malcolm says, not only bloody but 'luxurious, avaricious, false, deceitful, sudden, malicious, smacking of every sin that has a name.' And in the end his ruin seems almost complete. Let us explain the nature of this astounding transformation in his character.

Scholastic metaphysicians refer problems of the static order to the principle of substance and accidents, and those of the dynamical order to the principles of matter and form, potency, and act. This last principle—the central theory of Aristotle adopted by scholasticism—is especially important for our purposes here, because, as De Wulf remarks, 'there is no other way of explaining change than by regarding reality as consisting of act and potency.' [37] Before anything can pass from one state into another, it must have *in potency* what it finally becomes *in act*. '*Actuality* is, therefore, any present perfection, any degree of being which really exists; *potency* is the aptitude for receiving another degree.' The scholastics, it must be observed, 'extend this theory into fields undreamed of by Aristotle. They apply it to all contingent beings, corporeal and incorporeal, and make it synonymous with determinant and determinable, which affect all the compositions of changing being.' When one corporeal substance changes to another, the 'two terms of the process' must have a common element called prime matter ('principle of determination, potency'), which receives the impress of a specific element called substantial form (actuality). Thus in actualizing its potentialities, 'corporeal substance clothes itself in unceasing and always changing determinations. . . . This couple of potency and act is found everywhere in the fundamental composition of substance and accident, matter and form, essence and existence.'

Now when this metaphysical principle is applied to the incorporeal element of the human being, we arrive at the conception of a person or individual ego, an 'indivisible substance (potency), in which are rooted an infinite number of principles of operation (act).' And in moral philosophy the principle resolves itself into the concepts of *essentia* and *esse,* that is to say, into *essence* and *existence* (or *being*). In what, then, consists the *essence* of that moral creature, man, by virtue of which he is called *human?* The essence of his humanity is that he is endowed with consciousness, with a reasonable soul, and with the liberty and ability to control the end which he pursues. This end, as we have already seen, can only be his good. To will the good, and all good, is the supreme purpose of all men. 'Now this *essence* has or receives *existence* or *being*. Existence is the final determination, in relation to which essence is potentiality and non-being. *Existence* is the actuation *par excellence,* which cannot be reduced to any other kind of actuation.' In other words, *existence* is the realization *in act* of all the potentialities in the essence of the rational and moral creature, man. This profound 'becoming' must be carefully distinguished from an 'accidental "becoming," ' which is nothing more than the actuation of those potentialities with which the individual person is endowed, or a development of personality.

Now the precise nature of good and evil is, therefore, apparent. The good, or a good, is any present perfection of *existence* or *being;* and evil is the lack of *being* in any degree. Each thing has as much good as it has *being,* or as much evil as it wants fullness of *being*. Man is moral and human, and therefore good, in proportion to his realization *in act* of his rational nature—in proportion to his fullness of *being;* he is evil in proportion to his lack of *being*. Evil is not a positive thing, set in opposition to good; it is negative and barren, implying a privation or deficiency of good (I. 5. 1, 3). Likewise, says St. Thomas, 'we may speak of good and evil in actions as of good and evil in things: every action has goodness, in so far as it has *being;* it is evil, or lacking in goodness, in so far as it

122

is deficient in something that is due to its fullness of *being*.' Since man is a reasonable being, every evil act of his is that which lacks in some measure the quantity determined by reason (I–II. 18. 1). Every sin, therefore, may be said to be contrary to nature (I–II. 78. 3). And since it is the very *essence* of man to act in accordance with his nature and to 'will always the good or an apparent good as an end,' it follows that, though his *being* may diminish toward the vanishing point, there must always be some good left in him (I–II. 85. 2). Thus while man's consciousness reports his ego constant and his *essence* continuously human, his *being* alters, changes, and fluctuates as he passes from good to evil or *vice versa*. This is the most profound 'becoming' of which man is capable.

Such alteration or 'becoming' is witnessed in the individual by the act of conscience. This process, involving as it does the relation between man and both divine and natural laws, calls for elaboration. In God's ordering of his created universe we must observe two steps, namely, the reason of order and the execution of order. The type of things ordered toward an end in the mind of God may properly be called Providence; the execution of the providential design is Government. As to the design of government, God governs all things immediately, and nothing escapes from him as universal cause. But in the matter of execution of design, he governs through a mediate chain of secondary causes inherent in the nature of things created and under the supervision of certain orders of superior and inferior intelligences. We have observed elsewhere the execution of order in operation.[38] Now let us examine more closely into the reason of order. Just as the type of Divine Wisdom, creating all things, says St. Thomas, 'has the character of exemplar or idea,' so the type of Divine Wisdom, 'as moving all things to their due end, bears the character of law.' Accordingly, 'Eternal Law is nothing else than the type of Divine Wisdom, as directing all actions and movements' (I–II. 93. 1); 'it is the plan of government in the Chief Governor' (I–II. 93. 3). All other plans of government, therefore, must be derived from the Eternal Law. 'It is evident, for example, that all created things must partake somewhat of the Eternal Law, in so far as, namely, from its being imprinted upon them, they derive their respective inclinations to their proper ends and acts. Now among all others, the rational creature, man, is subject to Divine providence in the most excellent way possible; it has a share of Eternal Reason, whereby it has a natural inclination to its proper end and act, and this participation of the Eternal Law in the rational creature is called Natural Law.' Man is thus provided with the 'light of natural reason—the imprint of the Divine light—whereby he is able to discern what is good and what is evil, which is the function of the Natural Law' (I–II. 91. 2). These precepts of the Natural Law, which are the 'first principles of human actions,' are deposited in a sort of 'ineradicable habit or law of the mind,' called Synderesis (I–II. 94. 1). 'Whence Synderesis is sometimes said to incite to good and murmur at evil, inasmuch as through these unchangeable notions man proceeds to discover and to judge of what he has discovered' (I. 79. 12).

But more properly speaking, the application of this knowledge of right and wrong to particular instances is the act of Conscience, 'for conscience is knowledge applied to particular cases.' As a man develops toward good, therefore, 'his conscience is said to incite, to witness, to excuse, or to bind'; but as he deteriorates toward evil, it also 'accuses, rebukes, and torments' (I. 79. 13). Thus man naturally partakes of the eternal law both 'by way of knowledge and by way of an inward motive principle' (I–II. 93. 6). But 'both ways are imperfect, and to a certain extent destroyed, in the wicked; because in them the natural inclination to virtue is corrupted by vicious habits, and the natural knowledge of good is darkened by passions and habits of sin' (I–II. 93. 6). 'Your theologian considers sin chiefly as an offense against God,' *i.e.*, against the Eternal Law; the moral philosopher, on the other hand, emphasizes the aspect of its being something contrary to reason, *i.e.*, a violation of the Natural Law (I–II. 71. 6, *ad* 5). In either case conscience acts in accordance with the same first principles. We are interested here only in the approach of moral philosophy.

## VI

These philosophical principles, it seems to me, may well serve as guides to a partial understanding of Macbeth's spiritual experiences after the first murder. Between the occasion of his coronation and the opening of Act III, a considerable period of time has elapsed, representing a dreary reign of several weeks [39] accompanied by violent upheavals in Macbeth's inner life. He has achieved the supreme temporal good which his self-love demanded, and he may rest assured that no man is likely to question the means of attaining it. Confidence of the nobles has established him in power; the loyalty of friends and supporters has confirmed his honors. Nothing external seems to threaten greatly the ultimate success of his venture. But it now appears that in murdering Duncan he has reckoned without due consideration of his own essential nature: he has violated the precepts of the natural law deposited in him, and these first principles of human action maturate the drive of conscience which condemns the deed and witnesses to the shrinking of his being.

Macbeth's mind is in a state of great confusion regarding the processes taking place within him. The profound disturbance in the essential nature of the man expresses itself, psychologically speaking, in a horrible fear and torture of the mind assailing the

126

individual and in the affliction of terrible dreams that shake him nightly. Wracking passions, frayed nerves, and inordinate apprehension of the imagination have so impeded his reason that he conceives of Banquo's knowledge and possible suspicion as constituting the primary source of his distemper and the only threat to his peace. In Banquo his fears stick deep; under Banquo's royalty of nature, wisdom, and dauntless temper of mind, his genius is rebuked as it is said Mark Antony's was by Caesar. Elimination of Banquo would surely restore his ravished peace. And that he is not clearly conscious of the unreason inherent in these considerations, is indicated by the fact that his will does resolve upon the destruction of Banquo.

But here again we must grant him a complexity, or at least a confusion, of motives. He is somewhat aware also of the elemental cause of his dismal experience. The natural good in him compels the acknowledgment that, in committing the unnatural act, he has filed his mind and has given his eternal jewel, the soul, into the possession of those demonic forces which are the enemy of mankind. He recognizes that the acts of conscience which torture him are really expressions of that outraged natural law, which inevitably reduces him as individual to the essentially human. This is the inescapable bond that keeps him pale, and this is the law of his own nature from whose exactions of devastating penalties he seeks release:

127

> Come, seeling night . . .
> And with thy bloody and invisible hand
> Cancel and tear to pieces that great bond
> Which keeps me pale.

He conceives that quick escape from the accusations of conscience may possibly be effected by utter extirpation of the precepts of natural law deposited in his nature. And he imagines that the execution of more bloody deeds will serve his purpose.* Accordingly, then, in the interest of personal safety and in order to destroy the essential humanity in himself, he instigates the murder of Banquo. This act does not, of course, bring the peace which he desires. But its immediate effect is so far to numb his conscience that he is encouraged and confirmed in his bloody course:

> My strange and self-abuse
> Is the initiate fear that wants hard use:
> We are yet but young in deed.

In the meantime, Macbeth's conscience also asserts boisterously the radical change in his being. The negative character of his accomplishment fills the individual with dismay: the crown attained by crime is fruitless, the royal scepter in his gripe is barren, and he has put rancours in the vessel of his peace only for Banquo's issue. The fever of an evil life so shakes him that he envies Duncan the quietness of a grave. The bond of confidence which once linked him in a

* For a similar interpretation, see Adams, *op. cit.*, p. 200 ff.

beautiful relationship to his wife is broken; he is strong or reckless enough to execute his second murder without her aid. Diminution of the man's being is evidenced by a curious withdrawal from humankind; the divine light of reason in him so thickens that he no longer feels himself at one with the rest of humanity, and he is more and more thrown back upon his own counsels formulated by self-love. For his own good, all causes shall give way. He loses confidence in even friends and loyal supporters and keeps servants fee'd in all their houses. The good in him has so dwindled that he can imagine and desire a universal destruction without a qualm; if only his own peace and safety may be assured, let the frame of things disjoint and both the worlds, of good and evil, suffer. And after the murder of Banquo he recognizes the true status of his being: it is possible, he conceives, for him to turn about and renew attempts to actuate the potentialities of his essence, *i.e.,* to control passion and develop rationality; but the tendency to crime has fastened itself upon him and renders continuance in his present course easier and more desirable:

> I am in blood
> Stepp'd in so far that, should I wade no more,
> Returning were as tedious as go o'er.

His determination is strengthened to destroy his own being and to root out that natural good in his nature

129

which rouses conscience to acts of condemnation. And he so far succeeds that he is able to progress to other crimes swiftly and with but scant deliberation upon their enormity or consequences:

> Strange things I have in head, that will to hand;
> Which must be acted ere they may be scanned.

## VII

Irrationality and rioting passions, fostered by crime and selfish desire, now lord it over the essential rationality of his nature. Seeking contact with external evil, demonic forces symbolized by the Weird Sisters, the individual is led to believe that only a more bloody, bold, and resolute course can recreate that harmonious accord with all reality which he has destroyed. Consequently, the very firstlings of his heart become the firstlings of his hand; there is now no more boasting like a fool, no completely rational consideration of safety or of internal and external consequences of dread exploits. He progresses with incredible swiftness and violence toward the end which he has set for himself: namely, a sort of negative peace which must follow habitual violation of his essential humanity. Without immediate rational cause, for example, he surprises the castle of Macduff, seizes upon Fife, and gives to the edge of the sword his wife, his children, and all unfortunate souls that trace him

130

in his line. During the terrifying weeks which follow
this crime, Scotland groans under the yoke of his tyr-
anny; each new day a gash is added to her wounds.
As Macduff says:

> Each new morn
> New widows howl, new orphans cry, new sorrows
> Strike heaven on the face, that it resounds
> As if it felt with Scotland and yell'd out
> Like syllable of dolour.

The kingly graces, such as justice, verity, temper-
ance, stableness, honesty, mercy, devotion, and pa-
tience, fall away from him; and this negation of good
in him permits him to become luxurious, avaricious,
false, deceitful, sudden, malicious, smacking of every
sin that has a name. Macduff concludes:

> Not in the legions
> Of horrid hell can come a devil more damn'd
> In evils to top Macbeth.

But he gains no satisfying peace because his conscience still obliges him to recognize the negative
quality of evil and the barren results of wicked action.
The individual who once prized mutable goods in the
form of respect and admiration from those about him,
now discovers that even such evanescent satisfactions
are denied him:

> And that which should accompany old age,
> As honor, love, obedience, troops of friends,
> I must not look to have; but, in their stead,

131

Curses, not loud but deep, mouth-honor, breath,
Which the poor heart would fain deny, and dare not.

But the man is conscious of a profound abstraction of something far more precious than temporal goods. His being has shrunk to such little measure that he has lost his former sensitiveness to good and evil; he has supped so full with horrors and the disposition of evil is so fixed in him that nothing can start him. His conscience is numbed so that he escapes the domination of fears, and such a consummation may indeed be called a sort of peace. But it is not entirely what he expected or desires. Back of his tragic volitions is the ineradicable urge toward that supreme contentment which accompanies and rewards fully actuated being; the peace which he attains is psychologically a callousness to pain and spiritually a partial insensibility to the evidences of diminished being. His peace is the doubtful calm of utter negativity, where nothing matters. The death of his wife cannot touch him with either grief or regret; she should have died hereafter. All who have died before were fools, because life can hold nothing of positive value for any man; it is merely a succession of dreary and meaningless tomorrows:

> Life's but a walking shadow, a poor player
> That struts and frets his hour upon the stage
> And then is heard no more: it is a tale
> Told by an idiot, full of sound and fury,
> Signifying nothing.

132

In this universal negation he approaches the border-land of spiritual annihilation. And this is the ultimate tragedy of Macbeth.

This spectacle of spiritual deterioration carried to the point of imminent dissolution arouses in us, however, a curious feeling of exaltation. For even after the external and internal forces of evil have done their worst, Macbeth remains essentially human and his conscience continues to witness the diminution of his being. That is to say, there is still left necessarily some natural good in him; sin cannot completely deprive him of his rational nature, which is the root of his inescapable inclination to virtue. We do not need Hecate to tell us that he is but a wayward son, spiteful and wrathful, who, as others do, loves for his own ends. This is apparent throughout the drama: he never sins because, like the Weird Sisters, he loves evil for its own sake; and whatever he does is inevitably in pursuance of some apparent good, even though that apparent good is only temporal or nothing more than escape from a present evil. At the end, in spite of shattered nerves and extreme distraction of mind, the individual passes out still adhering admirably to his code of personal courage, and the man's conscience still clearly admonishes that he has done evil. Of all men he would have avoided Macduff, because his soul is too much charged already with Macduff's blood.

Moreover, he never quite loses completely the liberty of free choice, which is the supreme *bonum naturae* of mankind. But since a wholly free act is one in accordance with reason, in proportion as his reason is more and more blinded by inordinate apprehension of the imagination and passions of the sensitive appetite, his volitions become less and less free. And this accounts for our feeling, toward the end of the drama, that his actions are almost entirely determined and that some fatality is compelling him to his doom. This compulsion is in no sense from without —though theologians may at will interpret it so—as if some god, like Zeus in Greek tragedy, were dealing out punishment for the breaking of divine law. It is generated rather from within, and it is not merely a psychological phenomenon. Precepts of the natural law—imprints of the eternal law—deposited in his nature have been violated, irrational acts have established habits tending to further irrationality, and one of the penalties exacted is dire impairment of the liberty of free choice. Thus the Fate which broods over Macbeth may be identified with that disposition inherent in created things, in this case the fundamental motive principle of human action, by which providence knits all things in their proper order. Macbeth cannot escape entirely from his proper order; he must inevitably remain essentially human. The Fate which impels him is therefore always contingent, depending ultimately upon the degree of actuation which, by acts of free choice, he succeeds in giving to the potentialities of his essence.[40] His being has shrunk almost to the vanishing point, but the slight residuum of liberty of free choice at the end confirms our conclusion that Macbeth is, in the fullest sense of the term, the architect of his own fortunes. One may well stand in awe of such a being, indissolubly linked in essence to the natural and divine forces which govern the universe; and one may exult in the possibility of his exercising free volition even to his own salvation or destruction. We may pity the individual's bewilderment, suffering, and misdirected struggles for happiness; but the man's infallible response to the appearance of good must arouse our respect and admiration.

In this manner, it seems to me, principles of scholastic philosophy have exerted a formative influence upon Shakespeare's conception of Macbeth's changing character. We have indicated a sharp distinction between Macbeth as essential man and Macbeth as individual personality, though these aspects of the artistically unified character represent merely an application of the principle of potency and act to incorporeal reality in two planes, as it were. The substance of Macbeth's personality is that out of which tragic heroes are fashioned; it is endowed by the dramatist with an astounding abundance and variety of potentialities. And it is upon the development of these potentialities that the artist lavishes the full energies of his creative powers. Under the influence of swiftly altering environment which continually furnishes or elicits new experiences and under the impact of passions constantly shifting and mounting in intensity, the dramatic individual grows, expands, develops to the point where, at the end of the drama, he looms upon the mind as a titanic personality infinitely richer than at the beginning. This dramatic personality in its manifold stages of actuation is an artistic creation. The artist who produced it as such was indifferent to moral considerations; the critic who would estimate its dramatic effectiveness must, therefore, ignore ethical criteria. The present study, however, is not greatly concerned with Macbeth's personality, except in so far as its development seems to throw light upon that more profound 'becoming' to which the essential man is subject. In essence Macbeth, like all other men, is inevitably bound to his humanity: the reason of order, as we have seen, determines his inescapable relationship to the natural and eternal law, compels inclination toward his proper act and end but provides him with a will capable of free choice, and obliges his discernment of good and evil. The first principles of human action deposited in his nature are applied in the light of natural reason to specific instances, and this knowledge of right and wrong so applied becomes the act of conscience. As he grows in crime his being, or the actuation of his essence, diminishes until the natural good in him has almost disappeared; and evil, or the negation of good, is wit-

136

nessed to by the torture of conscience. This concept of the essential nature of man is evidently a moral concept, evolved through centuries of philosophical thinking in the realm of moral philosophy. The lines of its genesis stretch back to Aristotle, Plato, the Neo-Platonists, Christ, and others, but the plenary formulation of it must be attributed to the mediaeval scholastics. Moral philosophy of the Renaissance is almost entirely derivative and lacking in originality;[41] its statements of first principles have, therefore, not escaped rigid discipline at the hands of scholastic philosophers and their predecessors. Macbeth the man is, accordingly, not of Shakespeare's creating. But in successfully fusing this inherited and generally accepted concept of essential man with the dramatic personality of Macbeth, Shakespeare has created not only an effective dramatic figure but a magnificent tragic character of the Renaissance, which can be understood and ultimately criticized only by reference to defined standards of moral philosophy.*

* Scheme of the situation:

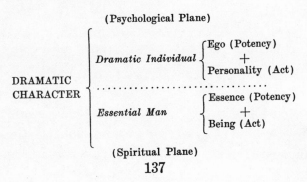

*Quid enim aliud est natura quam deus et divina ratio toti mundo partibusque eius inserta?*

LUCIUS ANNAEUS SENECA

# CHAPTER V

## THE AGE: PLATONISM

I

In the meantime other philosophical traditions—superimposed upon, or fused with, the scholastic inheritance—were tugging at the consciousness of this perturbed age, demanding recognition and hospitality. Here Platonism and Neo-Platonism, transmogrified by centuries of Oriental and Western manhandling, vied for supremacy with Aristotelianism, both Greek and scholastic. Stoicism rediscovered made its usual 'accommodation' to dominant pressures and injected its principles into the most singular combinations. Atomism, Epicureanism, Cynicism, and Pythagorean doctrines of numbers suffered a recrudescence and achieved astounding permutations in contact with Christianity, Egyptian and Chaldean theosophy, Persian magic, Indian gymnosophy, and Hebraic mythology.[1] Out of the syncretism of this welter of knowledge emerged the Renaissance conception of 'Platonic' pan-psychism—hylozoism, pantheism, empirical vitalism, spiritualized naturalism, or whatnot [2]—which begot and sustained a malformed prog-

141

eny of occult sciences. But in the formulation of this
curious 'Platonism' of the humanistic period, we
must observe, the most stimulating of the borrowed
systems were those bearing the features of the Stoic
and Neo-Platonic tradition.

II

Stoicism came to the Renaissance directly from
original sources, it is true, but also mediately through
devious channels as an element absorbed in other traditions. One may recall that it had postulated the
identity of primary matter and immanent deity; all
phenomena are manifestations of an interpenetrat-
ing Generative Reason and are bound by the inexo-
rable law of Providence. Man is a microcosm whose
morality consists in the realization of his rational nature and whose 'natural religion' expresses itself as
imperturbability and rationalized action. Pantheistic
conceptions allowed him to declare the existence of
the gods, together with an endless chain of 'daemons'
—both good and bad—who serve as intermediaries
between gods and men. His soul is immortal.[3] Now
when primitive Christianity came to formulate its
own philosophical principles, it could not escape dependence upon many doctrines of the Stoa.[4] The hu-
manitarianism, moral idealism, and natural religion
of Stoicism took such firm root in the Christian system that neither Augustine nor mediaeval scholastics

nor sixteenth-century reformers could ignore them. Indeed, as Wenly has it, 'Because the Stoa made philosophy *moral* philosophy and, at the same time, linked it with profound speculative problems, no limit can be set to its leaven within the undivided Church.'[5] And this leavening of Stoicism within Christianity became, of course, a heritage of the Renaissance.

A kind of sublimated Stoicism, moreover, transmuted in the alembic of artistic minds and fused with Neo-Platonism and other elements, found expression in the literature of the Middle Ages. The works of Cicero, Virgil, and Seneca represent the Latin efforts to assimilate and illuminate Stoic doctrines; and it was these writers who initiated, directly or indirectly, profound impulses in the mediaeval mind to creation. Macrobius combines Stoic cosmology with Platonism,[6] and Boethius reveals traces of Stoic determinism and natural religion.[7] And it was these philosophers who exerted a magistral power over Chaucer[8] and other mediaeval writers. Thus Stoic influence, carried in the stream of literary tradition, came in the Renaissance to coalesce with that Stoicism received directly from 'rediscovered' Seneca and Cicero and from the Greek Stoics.[9] But we must admit here that it was the hylozoic pantheism of the original tradition, revived and modified by a variety of contacts, which impressed itself most strongly upon the sixteenth-century mind and which finally, in that turbid mixture called Renaissance 'Platonism,' suppressed the dualistic motives inherent in Neo-Platonism proper.[10]

### III

Renaissance pan-psychism, however, was primarily of Neo-Platonic origin. Neo-Platonism had conceived, it will be remembered, of the world as emanating from the unknowable Absolute through successive stages of activity until the Light of the emanating World-Soul is lost in matter, which it informs and shapes. Two distinct realms are therefore postulated: namely, the supersensuous world, the ground of which is an 'intelligible matter' containing implicitly the forms of all things, and the reflected world of sense with its underlying 'corporeal matter' which, in conjunction with forms, is in a state of change and movement. In the Philonian attempt to resolve this implied dualism between God and the world, Platonic Ideas are transformed into the thoughts of God or archetypal, creative forces, sometimes identified with the Greek gods, daemons, and Jewish angels.[11] They are personified by later Neo-Platonists into a hierarchy of intelligences arranged in a dependent order from gods of the intelligible world down through a graduation of angels, archons, and daemonic powers, whose function it is to create, animate, and supervise all phenomena of the natural world according to laws prescribed by the World-Soul. Thus the universe is produced, all its diversities and oppositions unified, and its every activity governed by some manifestation of Spirit. In last analysis, Neo-Platonism is essentially a 'spiritual monism.'[12] Such doctrines and their corollaries we shall have to consider more fully later on, but for the present we are interested mainly in the dissemination of the Neo-Platonic tradition, its inter-relations with other traditions, and in its transmission into the Renaissance.

Undoubtedly Neo-Platonism, like Stoicism, exerted a powerful influence upon the primitive formulations of Christian doctrine and also upon the anti-scholastic systems of the Middle Ages. Augustine, for example, was acquainted with the Alexandrian mystics, with Plotinus, Apuleius, and Porphyry. He denied the emanative and monistic tendencies of Neo-Platonism but assimilated in his own thinking such conceptions as the ineffability of God and an exemplarism involving the seminal reasons.[13] His absorption in the scholastic tradition and the return of reformers to him for inspiration insured the transmission of Augustinian Neo-Platonism directly and indirectly into the sixteenth century. Meanwhile, moreover, the Middle Ages saw an efflorescence of Latin Neo-Platonism combined with mysticism and Averroism in opposition to scholasticism. Pseudo-Dionysius had adopted many doctrines of Plotinus and Proclus together with the allegorical mysticism of the Alexandrians, but he refused to countenance monism.[14] Macrobius, however, espoused with open mind certain emanative and monistic principles, which he is said to have combined with Neo-Pythagorean number-symbolism.[15] And John Scotus Eriugena evolved, after the manner of Proclus, a system involving the emanation of Divine Substance through four stages into the world of sense, where everything manifests the immanence of 'Theophanies.'[16] Following him, Neo-Platonists of the thirteenth century further elaborated the mystical aspects of emanation and, under the stimulus of Averroistic monopsychism,[17] developed monism into something resembling pantheism.[18] And this 'side-stream or undercurrent' of Neo-Platonic tradition, though not as congenial to the mediaeval mind as scholasticism, trickled its contents through Nicolas of Cusa [19] and others into the compound that was Renaissance Platonism.

In 1438 Georgios Gemistos Plethon came bustling to Florence, carrying with him a wealth of Greek cosmology, the speculative mysticism of a 'bastard Neo-Platonism,' and a fantastic plan which should unify the Christian Churches. The system proposed was a sort of 'universal theism.' Here Platonic Ideas are materialized or personified into a hierarchy of intellectual beings arranged in a logical order descending from Zeus through three series of divine intelligences —named after certain gods of the Greek pantheon— to spirits of planets and stars, various orders of daemons, and finally to men and the souls of material things.[20] Thus it was the pantheism of Plethon's system—the spectacle of a mystic world peopled throughout with divine presences—which stimulated his beauty-loving disciples and insured the swift dissemination of 'Platonism' in the Renaissance.

Then Marsilius Ficinus, head of the Platonic Academy at Florence, evolved an obfuscate system of thought dedicated to the worship of Divine Plato. As everybody knows, he gave to the Renaissance in Latin translation the complete works of Plato and Plotinus, some magical writings of Porphyry and Proclus, the *Hierarchies* of Dionysius, and the *Mysteries of the Egyptians* attributed to Iamblichus. He did not realize the function of Ideas in Plato's system or the implications of monistic emanation in Plotinus. It was rather the mysticism and poetic mythology of Plato which fired his imagination, and these he interpreted in the light of Neo-Platonism. His vague and misty thinking reduced the universe to a sublime theophany.[21] Such uncritical and impassioned thinking, indeed, was common in the humanistic period, an age delicately sensitive to even the most shadowy beauty. But with the separation of theology and philosophy, it was Francesco Patrizzi and his followers who combined Neo-Platonic conceptions of emanation with Neo-Pythagorean and Stoic doctrines and brought 'naturalistic monism' to its highest development.

They identified God with the world and emphasized the beauty and infinity of the universe as a manifestation of deity.[22]

And then came Pico della Mirandola, visioning a conciliation of classical and Christian traditions and projecting a work which should demonstrate the 'harmony of all philosophies in Christianity.' He never completed the fantastic project, but the key to his problem of discovering the 'quintessence of truth' in all systems was to be found, he believed, in the Jewish Cabbala. This curious compound of 'Hebrew traditions, Alexandrian myths, Asiatic fancies, and Christian doctrines,' he accordingly studied and translated.[23] He affirmed that in the Cabbala was to be found more Christianity than Judaism: 'he discovered in it proof for the doctrine of the Trinity, the Incarnation, the divinity of Christ, the heavenly Jerusalem, the fall of the angels, the order of the angels, purgatory and hell-fire; in fact the same gospel which we find in St. Paul, Dionysius, St. Jerome and St. Augustine.' [24] But what appealed to him most strongly, no doubt, was the Neo-Platonic conception of emanation which pervades the system. For, according to the Cabbala, the whole universe flows from an entirely mysterious Divine Being through four successive worlds, each created and sustained by a series of ten masculine and feminine intelligences or potencies. And man is the 'heavenly image' of such a universe, whose body and soul have imprinted upon them the marks of the entire creative process and contain the reflections or germs, as it were, of all knowledge and perfection. He is, therefore, superior to the angels and to the hierarchy of demons who inhabit the lowest world. And, finally, all this 'extension of divine substance' must be purified so that it may return to that Power from which it emanated.[25]

Now here is a system which must have impinged with tremendous import upon the early Renaissance mind prepared by Neo-Platonic and related traditions to receive it. Here came from the thirteenth century a synthesis, already fashioned to hand, of precisely those elements in which the imagination of the humanistic period reveled: Neo-Platonic emanations arranged according to Neo-Pythagorean number-symbolism, Jewish legend mingled with Dionysian and other traditions, mysterious and potent names of God arrived at by intricate permutation of letters,[26] Alexandrian mysticism, animism, pantheism, a splendid fusion of Hellenism, Hebraism, and Christianity [27]—in short, a mélange of breath-taking concepts, mystic, strange, wonderful. It is not surprising therefore that, when John Reuchlin brought Greek culture from Italy to aid in his initiation of the German Reformation, both speculative and wonder-working Cabbalism should have flown with him.[28] His treatises,[29] presenting this theosophy as 'the symbol of Divine revelation,' were eagerly welcomed by the thinkers and reformers of his time; and their contents, transmitted in various forms through the works of Cornelius Henry Agrippa, Robert Fludd and others, came to 'permeate all branches of sixteenth-century philosophy, life, and literature.' [30]

## IV

One deduction may now be made with confidence: Renaissance 'Platonism' was a heady concoction, calculated to obstruct clear thought and inflame the imagination. The supersensuous world and religious faith were grist for theological mills; it was the province of philosophy to study and admire the sensible world, *i.e.*, nature and its implications. There was accordingly much dithyrambic utterance about the World-Soul or World-Force, Unomnia, the Universal Intelligence or Divine All-Life, the infinite *natura naturans,* the efficient cause and dynamic principle of all things, who unfolds or prolongs himself into a spectacular nature, *natura naturata.* 'Xenophanes was supposed to have expressed static, and Heraclitus dynamic, pantheism; Anaxagoras had said: "All things are in all things; omnipotent, all producing divinity pervades the whole, therefore nothing is so small but that divinity lies concealed in it." ' [31] The Stoics had professed a hylozoic pantheism and the Neo-Platonists a spiritualized monism; the Cabbala had emphasized the emanation of the many from the unifying *En Soph;* Neo-Pythagoreans had numbered the mysteries. And nature or the 'universe' had now become for the humanistic period a visible manifestation of Divinity: it was either a reflection of the Divine Light where the whole is mirrored in each of its parts, or the beautiful mantle of the Creative Force, or an extension of his essence, or a living organism informed with his life-giving Spirit, or the instrument of God unified in its multifariousness by the infusion of his providence—sensitive, vital, spiritualized by Deity, animated in every smallest element, arranged according to number-mysticism, and dominated in all its life-activities by hierarchies of intelligences.[32] These are some of the most important elements of Renaissance pan-psychism.

One cannot expect writers of this period to be consistent in their thinking. They were uncritical eclectics, at once Christian, pagan, or otherwise, choosing from this or that tradition such elements as filled their needs or pleased their fancy. Bruno, for example, attributed the idea of a universal intelligence 'indiscriminately to the Pythagoreans, the Platonists, the Magi, Orpheus, Empedocles, and Plotinus.'[33] The God of Sir Thomas More's *Utopia* 'is a certayne godlie powre, unknowen, everlastyng, incomprehensible, inexplicable . . . dispersed through out all the worlde, not in bygnes, but in vertue and powre.'[34] But whether this concept is to be identified with Plato's World-Soul,[35] or with the Neo-Platonic Absolute, or the Cabbalistic *En Soph,* or with the Christian God, is by no means clear; it most probably represents a fusion of all of them. Phineas Fletcher conceived of a great Power or unifying All who, *by an exercise of will,* puts forth without diminution of his substance this undigested Ball and then as Light spreads cheerful rays through all the Chaos, framing the rest.[36] Thus the poet, blithely disregarding the contradiction in fundamental concepts maintained by history, conjured up a Power which, like the Neo-Platonic Absolute, should emanate the world—*not* properly, however, according to the necessity of his nature but, like the Christian God, by a fiat of will.[37] And so on. The age was pansophical without the power of nice discrimination. But it loved nature.

v

It also investigated nature and applied the corollaries of its naturalistic theory in experimentation designed to achieve practical ends. Since man is a microcosm in whose complexity the forms of total creation are lodged and united, scientists reasoned that he should be able not only to comprehend nature but to control and direct its activities. If, as the Cabbalists maintained, the world is an extension of Divine Substance, then the ground of nature's phenomena is a universal life-principle which informs all things. Accordingly your alchemist, understanding the sympathetic relationships of his spiritually unified system, should be able to manipulate by artificial means the 'virtues of things' (*i.e.,* the 'immortall Seede of worldly things, that God in the beginning infused into Chaos . . . by Universal extension'[38]) and, copying the processes of nature, accomplish the transmutation of one substance into another at will.[39] He might even liberate this virtue from the prison of earthly bodies and concentrate it in a purified substance called the Divine Elixir or Philosopher's Stone, which —working freely as it does in ethereal bodies—was thought to be capable of transmuting any substance into gold, restoring to perfection the sometimes weakened virtue in man, and of subjecting demonic powers to human direction.[40] In the compounding of medicines and treatment of diseases, therefore, the physician should consider these fundamental principles and, along with other scientists, rectify his practice by reference to the celestial bodies.[41] This process of managing for practical purposes the virtues of things was called natural magic.[42] If, as Neo-Platonists and Christians held, the activities of Nature are under the immediate dominance of demons or other spirits, then it was manifestly the province of any experimenter who would master nature to acquire knowledge of these ministering intelligences and to control them by prescribed means. One might, for example, form a league with the fallen angels of Christian theology or with the terrestrial daemons of paganism and, by means of incantations, suffumigations, and other ritualistic paraphernalia, control their wills and powers in the working of wonders. This was black magic or goety.[43] Or in his interference with the normal course of Nature the wise practitioner might, by means of clean living and by utilizing the inherent energy of mystic names and symbols, impress at will various orders of benefic daemons and even angels. And this was white magic or theurgy, of which the mediaeval notory art was a debased relation.[44] Thus in the humanistic period certain elements of Stoic, Neo-Platonic, Jewish, and Christian traditions combined and bloomed forth in a profusion of sciences: astrology and astrological medicine, alchemy, oneiromancy, necromancy, chiromancy, physiognomy, all sorts of divination and magic arts in bewildering variety. As Windelband says: 'Pico and Reuchlin brought them into connection with number-mysticism; Agrippa of Nettesheim adopted all the sceptical attacks against the possibility of rational science, in order to seek help in mystical illuminations and secret magic arts. Cardan proceeded in all seriousness to the task of determining the laws of these operations.'[45] Such was the 'scientific' outlook of Shakespeare's age; and no amount of condescending head-shaking over the 'superstition'[46] of the time or of exultation over the progress of 'true science' in succeeding centuries[47] can alter that fact. But the humanistic period did show experiment with nature.

154

VI

Disparagement by modernists, rejoicing in 'true science,' of such 'pseudo-scientific' theory and practices has tended to distract attention from the astonishing adaptability of this age to the profoundest needs of the artistic mind. Here was continuity with the past but little original or constructive speculation. Here were evolved no great systems which, like those of Plato, Aristotle, Descartes, or Kant, should mark the advance of philosophical thought. But the very profusion and chaos of conflicting traditions—where the rigidity of old orders was shattered, ancient systems disintegrated and their debris prepared for absorption into startling combinations, and the shifting elements of knowledge themselves were in process of being fused or reduced to such fluidity as to facilitate assimilation and adaptation to the new—constituted the ideal milieu for artistic production. Let but the poet-dramatist dip into the flow of sixteenth-century thought, for example, and any idea, or concept of action, or story which he might need was certain to be incredibly rich in associations acquired through a multiplicity of historical contacts—all now caught up in the fervid imagination of the time and already partially digested for his use. Let him absorb such materials into his own stream of consciousness and subject them to the transforming

155

and formative activities of his creative forces, and the emergent work of art was likely to be more profoundly complex but still unified, more complete, adequately expressive, and significant, than at any other time in the world's history. For the nature-philosophy of this period was in its own right a sort of poetry, in which the veil between the seen and the unseen was of gossamer thinness. It was metaphysical, symbolical, mystical, representing the development and concreting, as it were, of Plato's consciously poetic mythology and calculated to arouse awe in the presence of beauty and mystery. It embodied, in short, that 'miraculism' [48] which is probably the most essential quality of full-bodied poetry.

And this nature-philosophy of Renaissance Neo-Platonism had become, by 1605–10, the secondary groundwork of traditional cognition among Western peoples. It was at first merely a fashion or new mode of thought, assumed in opposition largely to contemporary scholasticism. But through more than two centuries of dissemination and intensive cultivation, it gradually acquired something resembling the aspects of a habit; that is to say, its concepts of man in relation to a pan-psychical nature, now become generally accepted and traditional, were superimposed in the Western mind upon the scholastic deposit and wherever possible forced into conformity with the basic principles of scholastic tradition. Along with the traditional thought-content, however, was trans-

mitted for a long time the style of displaying the
Greek, Italian, and other sources of it. But in some
cases this ostentation finally disappeared altogether,
and the free philosophy was absorbed and thoroughly
merged with other elements in the works of poets and
dramatists as if it had become, so to speak, a second
nature; it had become anonymous and communal.
Here again was a body of doctrines which an artist
might use without reference to specific origins; being
acquired by processes of traditional cognition, it was
his by right of inheritance and assimilation.

VII

Now in the latter part of his life Shakespeare came
to share also in this Neo-Platonic patrimony. Efforts
have been made, for example, to show his direct dependence in *Hamlet* upon certain pantheistic doctrines of Giordano Bruno.[49] But whether he knew
Bruno personally or studied the Italian's works themselves is not determinable. Nor is it important to demonstrate his immediate relationships to any writers
in the Neo-Platonic tradition. Everybody, including
Shakespeare, knew about 'the prophetic soul of the
wide world, dreaming on things to come'; and everybody was acquainted with the hierarchy of Neo-
Platonic daemons—as distinguished from the fallen
angels of Christian theology—which control the activities of nature and serve as mediators between

157

gods and men.[50] It is not therefore surprising to find that Shakespeare, who seems to have had an astonishing capacity for absorbing traditional materials without the exercise of any great scholarly efforts, should have employed the popular scientific theory of his time as the philosophical pattern of *The Tempest*.[51]

For this drama was composed (conjecturally *ca.* 1610) at the happy time when occult sciences based upon pan-psychical theory had achieved their culmination in England and at the moment when naturalistic science, which should finally supplant them in part, was just beginning to be articulate without having attained any devastating momentum.[52] Specifically, the science which he allowed to integrate the materials of this play is not black magic but white magic or theurgy, a body of pagan doctrines embodying natural magic which found purest expression in the *De mysteriis* of Iamblichus. How Shakespeare came to possess the contents of this work, or of others like it, is not clear; he may possibly have made firsthand investigations for himself, or he might have picked up, in conversations with such a scholar as Ben Jonson, a knowledge of its popular and widely disseminated concepts sufficient for his artistic purpose. At any rate, when the modern interpreter comes to demonstrate the functioning of theurgy as philosophical pattern of *The Tempest,* he finds it necessary to reconstruct that pure theurgy of the fourth century, together with its background, in order that for the modern mind the outlines of this system may stand out sharply defined and unblurred by centuries of tampering hands.[53] He may then propose to show, with some likelihood of success, that Prospero is the sacred personage or theurgist, *i.e.*, the scientist, who sets about controlling the activities of nature through the subjugation of its guardian spirits to his will. These purposes and these methods will be found to obtain in our following discussion of *The Tempest*.

*Ενα ιδοις αν εν πασᾳ γῃ ομοφωνον
νομον και λογον, οτι θεος εις παντων
βασιλευς και πατηρ, και θεοι παλλοι,
θεου παιδες, συναρχοντες θεῳ.*

MAXIMUS TYRIUS

# Chapter VI

## SACERDOTAL SCIENCE IN SHAKESPEARE'S
### *THE TEMPEST*

Shakespeare's *The Tempest* is an artistic creation which furnishes a perennial stimulus to the creative imagination of its audience. Divergent interpretations have at various times stamped it as pure romance, as realism, partial autobiography, symbolism, or as the allegorical representation of life and history.[1] One cannot help observing, however, that the characters portrayed in it have a tendency to escape complete definition; when confined within the limits of critical or scholarly theory, they are likely to diminish in stature and to lose much of their artistic exuberancy. Nor is the action more tractable. It seems to overflow the bounds of the ordinarily natural and to lose itself in a preternatural order which persistently resists delimitation. This ineffable quality must always characterize the true work of art. Nevertheless, it is not an inherent element of the crude materials elaborated by the artist's imagination. When available, therefore, this raw stuff of experience may be thought of as yielding itself readily to identification and partial analysis, even when it emerges as so subtle a thing as

163

the dramatist's conception of the universe and man's relation to it. Accordingly this present study is concerned neither with a criticism of *The Tempest* as a work of art nor with consideration of the discoverable source of its plot-elements.[2] Its general purpose is rather to examine and observe in operation certain philosophical concepts, inherited from the classical past, which Shakespeare employs as artistic pattern for *The Tempest*.

Before we can determine the philosophical pattern of *The Tempest,* it is necessary to establish the nature of certain figures and the precise quality of those external forces to which they are related. Throughout the drama peculiar emphasis rests upon Prospero the enchanter as sharply distinguished from Prospero the man; though the beneficent man is doubtless back of the action, the power through which he exercises his will over nature and other characters is for the most part preternatural. It is Prospero the enchanter who raises the tempest at the beginning of the play, renders himself invisible upon occasion, owns to a prescience which discerns some coming events, induces remorse and sleep in others; it is he who charms the bodies of his enemies into immobility or leads them as he wills by the sounds of magic harmony. He causes to appear magnificent spectacles which melt into thin air at his command. He professes to have bedimmed the noontide sun, called forth the mutinous winds, to have given fire to the rattling thunder; he has initiated earthquakes and has called forth spirits of the dead from their graves. All these wonders he seems to accomplish through the immediate instrumentality of certain orders of elvish spirits under the command of Ariel, who is himself subject to the enchanter's will. Ultimately, however, Prospero's power over these spiritual intelligences is derived from the judicious employment of certain arcane mysteries found in his books of magic. His magic robe and staff, airy charms and magic circles, together with his courting of the influence of stars, are effective only as they represent the application of forces liberated and accessible to him through the aid of his books.

Prospero's enchantments, however, are in no sense the products of Black Magic, nor are the ministers whom he employs the demons and devils of superstition or the fallen angels of Christian theology. Doctor Johnson, to be sure, would darken counsel by identifying the preternatural of this play with 'that system of enchantment which supplied all the marvellous found in the romances of the Middle Ages.'[3] Skottowe charges the dramatist with error in permitting Ariel, a creature of darkness, to perform his work in broad daylight.[4] Professor Bushnell, on the contrary, more sanely remarks:

Here there is no secret, black and midnight art; here there are no squeaking ghosts, no foul witches, no satanic revels or fairy intrigues; all Prospero's works are performed in the full light of the sun, with the harmonious cooperation of the forces of nature.[5]

Nevertheless, *The Tempest* offers for consideration two sorts or grades of enchantment. On the one hand, that damn'd witch Sycorax is said to have been guilty of manifold mischiefs and of sorceries too terrible to be reported. Because of one thing she did, her life was spared, however, and she was banished from Algiers to Prospero's island, where she gave birth to that demi-devil, Caliban. Her earthy commands were at one time laid upon Ariel; but because this delicate spirit refused her grand hests, she confined his substance, by the help of her more potent ministers, into a cloven pine. Through necromantic charms she could control the moon, make ebbs and flows, 'and deal in her command, without her power.' Her purposes are represented as being uniformly malignant. Prospero, on the other hand, is the wise philosopher-magician who employs beneficent spirits in the execution of benevolent purposes. In neither case is the enchantment involved to be identified with that Black Magic developed during the Middle Ages and transmitted to the Renaissance. It is the specific purpose of this study to demonstrate rather that the scientific pattern of *The Tempest*, which combines the sorcery of Sycorax and the enchantments of Prospero, represents that aspect of later Neo-Platonic philosophy known as sacerdotal science or theurgy.

Theurgy, as distinguished from goety or the black

art, is as ancient as the ceremonial religions of paganism. Wherever men have conceived of commerce with divinity in any form, conservators of the mysteries have practiced the equivalent of theurgy. It may be called a science or system of philosophy according to which an especially initiated priest is enabled, by means of incantations or other ceremonial business, to energize in the gods or to control other beneficent spiritual intelligences in the working of miraculous effects. Goety, on the other hand, is a black art, sometimes called the lowest manifestation of the sacerdotal science; its evil practitioner produces magic results by disordering the sympathetic relationships of nature or by employing to wicked ends the powers of irrational spirits. This distinction between illegitimate magic and the honorable science, for which the term *theurgy* was later devised, is common in classical antiquity;[6] but it is especially prevalent among certain Neo-Platonists of the so-called Alexandrian school. St. Augustine speaks of 'an art which they call either magic, or by the more abominable title necromancy, or the more honorable designation *theurgy.*'[7] Plotinus gives credence to a *goety* which employs for its effects the natural sympathy existing in a vitally unified universe,[8] but he will have nothing to do with theurgy.[9] Likewise Porphyry, while seeming to promise 'some kind of purgation of the soul by the help of theurgy,'[10] cannot help observing skeptically that its results are frequently trivial.[11] But it is Iamblichus who, in reply to Porphyry's strictures, distinguishes most clearly between goety and theurgy and offers the most precise and definitive exposition of theurgical operations.[12] Christianity, however, finally wipes out these distinctions and, in one respect, matures the prophecy of Eunapius: 'A fabulous and formless darkness shall tyrannize over the fairest things on earth.' [13] Following the lead of St. Augustine,[14] Christianity reduces the irrational, rational, and intellectual daemons of the Neo-Platonic system to the status of fallen angels or devils, and resolves accordingly both goety and theurgy into the miasmic sweep of Black Magic.

Consequently it is almost impossible to find any Renaissance writers who are willing to give an adequate exposition of the principles of theurgy or to offer a just estimate of its claims. This so-called 'white magic' is observed with suspicion and generally condemned along with other exhibitions of necromantic art. Cornelius Agrippa, for instance, rejects 'hanc fictitiam & palliatam Theurgiam' when he says that

saepissime sub nominibus Dei & Angelorum, malis daemonum fallaciis eam obstringi & licet eius ceremoniarum pars maxime, munditiam animi, corpori et rerum externarum vtensiliumque ostentet, immundos tamen spiritus & deceptrices potestates hanc exquiere, vt adorantur pro Diis . . . huius speciem esse artem Almadel, artem notoriam, artem

Paulinam, artem reuelationum & huiusmodi superstitionum plura, quae eo ipso sunt perniciosiora, quo apparent imperitis diuiniora.[15]

When in 1569 J. Sanford comes to translate Agrippa, he knows that 'the partes of ceremoniall Magicke be Goecie and Theurgie' [16] and that 'Porpherie who doth muche dispute of this Theurgie or Magicke of thinges divine doth finally conclude that with Theurgicall consecration man minde may be made apt to receaue Spirits and Angels'; [17] but being a Christian, he cannot countenance the practice. In 1584 Reginald Scot observes that there 'is yet another art, which is called Theurgie; wherein they work by good angels'; [18] but he finds that its nefarious practitioners are guilty of 'countrefet cousenage.' Fortunately for Shakespeare, however, treatises dealing with a pure theurgy not yet contaminated by Christian interpretation were made available by the activities of the Florentine Academy. In 1492 the humanist, Marsilius Ficinus, edited and translated the works of Plotinus together with Porphyry's *Life of Plotinus;* [19] in 1497 he published the *De mysteriis* attributed to Iamblichus— from which Porphyry's *Letter to Anebo* may be reconstructed [20]—and the *De sacrificio et magia* of Proclus.[21] In these works may be found the purest and most complete expression of theurgical principles. And undoubtedly Shakespeare had access in some way to their contents.[22] Let us consider, therefore, such expositions of the sacerdotal science as are presented by Proclus, Porphyry, and especially Iamblichus.

Neo-Platonism in general conceives of the world as emanating from God through several successive stages of activity. First, according to Plotinus, there is God the Absolute, the transcendant One, undetermined, unchangeable in essence, and plural only in his workings. This first Principle of divine activity expresses itself, according to the necessity of its essence, in a second sphere called Rational Soul (νοῦς), which is differentiated into the duality of thought and being. This rational spirit causes to emanate from itself Universal Soul (ψυχή'), which receives the world of Ideas from Spirit and uses them as archetypes after which it, as active principle, creates the cosmos, or world of sense. From Soul, therefore, proceed the formative powers of nature (φύσις), the individual souls of men, and the bright gods. From nature emanate daemons.[23] Thus as Soul descends into the world of generated things, its activities may be conceived of as finding direction along three lines: (1) through a brooding and unconsciously creating nature until the cosmos is produced immediately by the λόγοι σπερματικοί; (2) through the souls of man as they descend into material bodies; and (3) through a hierarchy of divine intelligences, extending from the gods through various orders of daemons into ultimate matter. Some such scheme, with certain expansions and variations, is implicit in the work of later Neo-Platonists. But Plotinus is mainly interested in the contemplation of a whole universe, spiritual and material, sensitized and bound together by one spirit into a single 'animal,' a part of which is man; gods and daemons have little part in the system. Later Neo-Platonists of a theurgical favor, however, are primarily concerned with the descent of Soul through gods and daemons, and through the spirits of men, into the world of sense. They emphasize the relationships between these latter manifestations and contemplate the possibility of man's assimilation to the gods, resulting in his exercise of such spiritual activities as the gods themselves are capable of. If the happy theurgist would escape the bonds of Fate and dominate the material world about him, he must first identify himself spiritually with the superior divine natures and so render himself capable of controlling the lesser divinities who immediately govern nature.[24]

For example, Iamblichus postulates two extremes of the divine genera, the beginning and the end: namely, the gods and human souls. To the gods, on the one hand, may be ascribed all essential good and the whole of that which is united in the world. They are firmly established, immovable, and separate; yet they are also the cause of all created essences, the initiators of all motion, and must be understood as common to all essence, power, and energy (I, v).[25] Intellect, or the demiurgic power of the universe, is always present with them in perfection (I, viii). Thus the completely unified gods may be thought of as emanating and governing a heterogeneous universe by the exercise of two distinct powers: namely, vivific and generative. And both powers are represented in the production of human beings. For human souls may be called the ultimate distribution into parts of the principle of life resident in the gods; but human bodies are among the most remote products of the generative powers of divine natures. In human souls, therefore, essential good is not present; good may be attained only through participation and habit (I, v). But when they descend into generation, human souls acquire such a composite nature that they are capable of understanding and communing with all created things (I, v). They possess a life and energy similar to that of all the forces which produced them and comprehend in themselves all essences and reasons, together with the forms or species of every kind (II, 2).

Now between these two extremes of divine genera, gods and men, we must conceive of two orders of media: namely, heroes and daemons. The order of heroes, produced like the human soul by the vivific powers of the gods, is suspended immediately from divine natures. The essence of heroes is, therefore, rational, and their powers are vivific. Occupying a place midway between gods and men, they perfect the life of souls and lead them from the world of things to the gods (I, v; II, 1). The order of daemons, on the other hand, is produced according to the generative powers of divine natures. The essence of daemons is perfective of mundane natures; their powers are primarily productive and operative (I, v). That is to say, as the world emanates from the gods through successive stages of activity, the whole process is presided over immediately and consummated by a hierarchy of daemons. Not only do these mediators transmit the demiurgic powers of the gods into the world of generated things, but they also serve as ministers of the gods in the operations of nature (I, xx; II, i). It is their immediate function to rule over and guard the elements of the universe, all individual bodies, and everything contained in the world, and to conduct all natural phenomena in accordance with the will of the gods (III, xv). Thus these middle genera, heroes and daemons, complete and make permanent the common bonds between gods and men (I, v). But we are for the present interested primarily in the nature and function of daemons.

From what has already been said, one may conclude that daemons are the ministers of Fate or Destiny. According to late Neo-Platonic philosophy, everything in the universe must be divided into two classes, the intellectual and the sensible, which correspond to two distinct kingdoms, the celestial realm of the gods and the sensible world of generated things. Since the latter is an emanation of the former, we may expect an exact parallelism between the two worlds; every relationship between material bodies is a reflection of an analogous relationship in the celestial spheres, and every body has stamped upon its essence the image, or sign, or symbol of its divine origin.[26] This doctrine of signatures is, as we shall see, a vital element in theurgy. Now the higher kingdom, which rules over both intellectuals and sensibles, may be called the realm of Providence; and the subordinate kingdom, which controls the sensible world alone, is the realm of Fate or Destiny. If we may define nature as 'that single unitary world-nature which creates, relates, and moves all material bodies,'[27] then Fate may be identified with nature. As Proclus says:

Fate, therefore, is the Nature of this world, being an incorporeal essence. It presides over, and constitutes the life of bodies, in an essential manner; since it moves bodies not only externally and in accordance with time, connecting the motions of all things, even those separate in time and place; which also induces the participation of mortal beings with external natures, weaving them together, as they are naturally receptive.[28]

Thus Fate is not merely a connected causal series with Providence serving as ultimate cause; it is, as Boethius says, 'the disposition and ordinance inherent in movable things, by which Providence knits all things in their orders.'[29] But, as we have seen, dae-

174

mons are essentially assimilated to generation and operation in the world of sensible things, and as such they may rightfully be called the servants of Fate.

Not all daemons, however, have like powers and functions. Since they mediate between gods and the world, we must conceive of them as being arranged in a hierarchy, each rank having control of all inferior ranks. According to Olympiodorus, for instance, there are six genera of daemons placed under the gods:

The highest of these subsist according to *the one* of the gods, and is called an unific and divine genus of daemons. The next subsist according to the intellect which is suspended from deity, and is called intellectual. The third subsists according to the soul, and is called rational. The fourth according to nature, and is denominated physical. The fifth according to the body, and is called corporeal-formed. And the sixth, according to matter, and this is denominated material.

Or if one cares to classify them according to habitat, 'it may be said that some of these are celestial, others ethereal, others aerial, others aquatic, others terrestrial, and others subterranean.' [30] Or regrouping according to their degree of spirituality, we may reduce them to three genera: intellectual substances (celestial and ethereal), rational substances (aerial), and irrational substances (aquatic, terrestrial, and subterranean).[31]

Neo-Platonic opinion regarding whether daemons

have bodies and sensibility is divided. Iamblichus denies them any sort of bodies (I, 8; 11; 16) and affirms that, being spiritual substances, they are completely impassive and without passions (I, 10; 11).[32] Plotinus claims that, though they do not possess bodies composed of corporeal matter, still their essence may be identified with a sort of intelligible or 'spiritual matter' which enables them to participate in matter and to clothe themselves at will in airy or fiery bodies.[33] Consequently, they have senses and memory; they suffer through their irrational part and can hear and answer petitions.[34] Porphyry, among many others,[35] contends that all daemons have bodies composed of air or fire (I, 8); they have sensibility and experience a variety of emotions, particularly daemons of a low order, so that they suffer when touched.[36] Though they are not provided with organs of generation, irrational daemons are capable of reproducing their kind and of crossing with human beings.[37] All seem agreed, however, that they are able to assume at will whatever forms please their imaginations.[38] But the presence of daemons is normally indicated to men by certain characteristics of their *phasmata* or luminous appearances. Both daemoniacal and heroical self-visive spirits have a beauty in definite forms, but the fire of daemons is definitely circumscribed by a distribution into parts, is effable, and does not astonish the sight of those who have seen more excellent natures (II, 4). When daemons appear, the whole air about them is not affected by their light; nor are they preceded, like other higher natures, by an effulgence which diffuses a splendor everywhere (II, 8). They rather present themselves to view with a turbid and unstable fire (II, 4), which waxes and wanes (II, 3), followed frequently by perturbation and disorder. Their movements seem to be more rapid than they really are (II, 4). Thus the *phasmata* of daemons have many essential characteristics in common with the *ignis fatuus*.

With this texture of the universe in mind, let us consider more closely the Neo-Platonic conception of goety and theurgy. Between these two there is not so much a difference in kind as a sharp definition according to degree; goety is an art, theurgy is a science which, though ultimately transcending the art, may and usually does compass its fundamental principles. The distinction is based, however, upon two entirely different aspects of human energizing; the one completely human, the other intellectual and supernormal. And these divergent activities, in turn, point to the fact that man is endowed with two souls. The lower soul, like the human body, is produced and governed by the motions of the world of sense. It is, therefore, mortal and cannot exist in separation from the body; it is caught in the meshes of Fate from which there is no escape. The higher soul, on the other hand, is derived from the intelligible gods. This principle of the human soul is eternal; it may completely

transcend the mundane order over which Fate rules;
it is capable of being united to the gods and of partici-
pating in their energy (VIII. 6, 7, 8). In the practice
of goetical art, therefore, only the normal powers of
men need be employed; in theurgical operations, the
intelligible soul departs from the world of sense and
energizes in mystic union with divine natures.

Plotinus, for example, finds that magic is the result
of a disturbance in the natural harmony of the universe. For the universe is a living organism, the parts
of which are bound together by sympathetic relationships under the direction of reason.[39] Now even the
ordinary wise man may achieve a certain understanding of the attractions and repulsions as they appear
about him in nature. But it is the wicked magician
who, by means of songs, invocations, figures, and
other incantations, shifts and abnormally concentrates the natural powers which things have to compel each other's love or hate.[40] The magic art, therefore, can produce only disorder and disturbance in
the delicate balance of the mundane order (IV, 7).
Hence, as Apuleius says,

By magical incantations rapid rivers may be made to run
back to their fountains, the sea be congealed, winds become
destitute of spirit, the sun be held back in his course, the
moon be forced to scatter her foam, the stars be torn from
their orbits, the day be taken away, and the night be de-
tained.[41]

When such marvels as these represent a disorganization in the world of generated things, they may be actually performed by the magician. But the celestial realms are not subject to the magic art; consequently, we must suppose with Psellus that such manifestations as blotting out the sun or tearing the stars from their orbits are nothing more than phantastic appearances.

It is quite apparent that goetical art cannot function without the aid of daemonic spirits, because every individual part of nature is under the immediate guardianship of its especially appointed daemon. It is also clear that material things are controlled immediately by only that lowest order of spirits called irrational daemons. In their capacity of contributing to wholes, even irrational daemons are superior to man; and when allowed to exercise their natural functions undisturbed, they are beneficent— though framed for evil because of their irrationality and proximity to matter. But having neither reason nor principle of judgment of their own, they may be commanded by that rational creature, man (IV, 2). By virtue of his rationality, therefore, the wicked magician finds it easy to subvert, disorganize, and misdirect the normal processes of nature: urged by selfish passion, he compels to his nefarious ends the irrational guardians of created things. From this unholy association, the irrational daemons emerge utterly depraved and evil; and the magician becomes, by contact with this irrational element in nature, more subject to passion and consequently more debased.

Your theurgist, on the other hand, aims primarily at union with the gods, and his theurgical practices may be regarded as a means of preparation for the intellectual soul in its upward progress. We must remember, however, that the gods are completely impassive; they incline neither toward the world of generated things nor toward the soul of man (I, 14; II, 17). It is necessary, therefore, for the soul to approach the gods; while still inhabiting the body, it must slough off passion and transcend its former life, exchanging it for a life in the gods (I, 12; IV, 2; VI, 6). Thus as the soul energizes according to another energy, it ranks no longer in the order of men but in that of the gods. Such union with higher natures does not depend upon philosophical thinking or reasoning (I, 21). These processes, together with personal purity and excellence of soul, may be antecedent causes (II, 11). But the ultimate union is achieved 'only by the due ritual fulfilment of the unspeakable acts which are beyond all intellection, and by the power of the unutterable symbols which are intelligible only to the gods' (II. 11).[42] Let us, therefore, consider the nature and power of arcane symbols.

Exponents of theurgy base their doctrine of signatures upon that parallelism existing between the noumenal and phenomenal worlds.[43] We have already seen how nature receives from the gods certain forms which, with the aid of daemons, it casts upon matter and so unfolds into being the world of sense (I, 21). It is, therefore, apparent that every material thing has stamped upon it, as by a seal, the impress of its divine origin. These signs or symbols may be imagined as active principles working under the direction of daemons, who transmit their power into material things. The theurgist does not understand these signatures of divinity; but by discovering them, he may be brought through their instrumentality into contact with the gods (II, 11). For example, the occult properties of such sensible forms as animals, flowers, and stones may lead the theurgist into union with divinity (III, 17).[44] And besides these manifestations in nature, the gods provide other signs of coming events or symbols of their will through such means as meteors and miraculous phenomena under the immediate direction of daemons (III, 16). The symbol may also be identified with ceremonial ritual, mystic words, or with ineffable names of the gods (VII, 4, 5). And men are capable of recognizing these symbols because 'we preserve in the soul collectively the mystic and arcane image of the gods, and through this we elevate the soul to the gods, and when elevated conjoin it as much as possible with them' (VII, 5).

Energizing perfectly or only partially in the gods, the scientific operator is enabled to perform his theurgical works with the aid always of divine natures. We must observe, however, that as the soul is drawn upward toward the gods, it passes successively through higher and higher planes of being and activity until it finally reaches the realm of the gods. The power of the practitioner, therefore, is graduated and must be more or less imperfect until the final stage is achieved. And the soul's elevation at any given moment may be gauged by reference to that order of divine natures—suspended in a hierarchy from the gods—which it controls (I, 15). For example, mere man may control irrational daemons in the practice of goetical art; but when his soul has been elevated to the point where he commands aerial daemons, then he is able to control mundane natures, not as man but as theurgist (IV, 2). He now makes use of greater mandates than pertain to himself as man (VI, 6). As his soul passes further through the spheres of ethereal and celestial daemons, his mystic powers become greater and more god-like. And finally, when he is completely assimilated to the gods, he becomes impassive like them and is able to exercise all the powers of the gods themselves (IV, 2). Through the power of symbols, presented to him from the gods by means of daemons (II, 15, 16, 18), he now becomes clairvoyant and prescient, understanding and announcing the will of the gods in all things (II, 3). Connected in this manner with the gods, the soul becomes more pure and beneficent. And as Iamblichus concludes:

> If, also, it elevates the reasons of generated natures, con-
> tained in it, to the gods, the causes of them, it receives power
> from them, and a knowledge which apprehends what has
> been, and what will be; it likewise surveys the whole of time,
> and the deeds which are accomplished in time, and is allotted
> the order of providentially attending to and correcting them
> in an appropriate manner (II, 3).

From this greatly simplified exposition we may conclude that theurgy is essentially a glorified theology and secondarily a science. It conceives clearly of a universe perfectly harmonized and unified by an all-pervading spirit, and emphasizes the splendid dignity and powers of the human soul in its alliance with all reality. But aside from that and more important for us here, it furnishes a bountiful legacy of myth and concept which the poetic mind apparently finds congenial and richly adaptable to its own purposes. Shakespeare, as we have suggested, has chosen to employ this classical concept of the theurgist's relation to animate nature as the philosophical pattern of *The Tempest*. If he emphasizes the science of theurgical works at the expense of more theological aspects of the system, that is in the interest of his artistic work as such. And if at times Christian conceptions seem to overlie the fundamental pattern, we shall find them inhering principally in the phraseology. Indications of folk-beliefs and the paraphernalia of contemporary Black Magic also appear for dramatic reasons in the play, but they are conciliated with the general pattern. Let us observe how concepts of the sacerdotal science work as integrating principles in *The Tempest*.

That foul witch Sycorax undoubtedly practiced goetical art, the lowest manifestation of the sacerdotal science. By virtue of her rationality as human being, she must have been able to command irrational daemons or invoke others and through them to disorder the sympathetic relationships in Nature. Her compelling charms were in some way associated with toads, beetles, and bats, and with wicked dew brushed with raven's feather from unwholesome fen. What the sorceries were, for which she was banished from Algiers, we do not know; but the fact remains that in her associations with irrational daemons she became debased to the point of cohabiting with one of them. Caliban was the product of that union—got, as Prospero says, by the devil himself upon the monster's wicked dam. Without being misled by Prospero's phrasing of this affair in terms of mediaeval Black Magic, we may logically conclude that Caliban's father was an aquatic daemon. The freckled whelp is not honored with a human shape, but he bears upon both mind and body the impress of his divine-human origin. Trinculo asks,

184

What have we here? a man or a fish? dead or alive? A fish: he smells like a fish; a very ancient and fishlike smell. A strange fish! . . . legged like a man! and his fins like arms! Warm, o' my troth.

And yet the water monster is also a land monster, who experiences a low order of human passions and in dreaming has visions of rich beauty ready to drop upon him. His brutish qualities indicate the desolate fusion of debased human with irrational daemonic nature.

It is reported, moreover, that Sycorax was strong enough to control the moon, make ebbs and flows, and deal in her (*i.e.*, the moon's) command without her power. That is to say, according to nature the regular rise and fall of oceanic waters is caused principally by lunar attraction; but Sycorax, by commanding those aquatic daemons whose province it is in any case to control immediately all states and movements of water, was able to produce ebbs and flows at will without reference to the moon at all. Through purely daemonic agency she disturbed natural processes to the extent of causing certain effects which are normally generated by a specially designated part of the whole. She 'controlled' the moon only in the sense that she achieved effects—*e.g.*, the moon's command: ebbs and flows—which nature intended only the moon to produce; and she accomplished her purpose through the instrumentality of forces divorced from the moon's direction, *i.e.*, without the moon's power.

In short, the moon's command in making ebbs and flows must always be immediately executed by irrational daemons; but the witch gained control of the moon's irrational ministers and through them created ebbs and flows when she pleased.

Her relations to Ariel are more obscure and involve an apparent contradiction. Ariel is reported to have been her servant, yet she could not command his will: when she laid her earthy commands upon him, the delicate spirit refused her grand hests. Enraged she called upon her more potent ministers and by their aid worked such sorcery upon him that his aerial substance was confined in a cloven pine. Such was the power of this charm that she herself was unable to undo it; dying, she left him there to suffer for a dozen years until Prospero released him. Here is a strange business. But the contradiction is no more than apparent. Here we must distinguish nicely between the invoking and the commanding of daemons. In general, aerial and ethereal daemons are deputized to inform men what they ought and ought not to do; they assist in just works and hinder such as are wicked (IV, 1; II, 7). Now the goetist, as man, may *invoke* even these excellent natures and secure their services in operations conformable to the symmetry of nature; but he cannot in any event *command* them, nor can he successfully *invoke* their aid to the accomplishment of evil (IV, 2). Only the theurgist is able to *command* these superior powers (IV, 2). It is quite evident, therefore, that Ariel's services to Sycorax, who merely invoked them, must have been limited to such operations as he could perform without violating his nature. But when she attempted to lay earthy *commands* upon him, the delicate spirit rebelled.

By exercising a powerful charm, however, she confined his substance in a tree. This torment she was able to consummate by invoking the corporeal powers of the universe, from which an involuntary gift of energy normally takes place (IV, 10). This gift is dependent upon the 'concord of similars and the contrariety of dissimilars' in the quick body of the universe (IV, 9). Thus in a sympathetically ordered world all natures and bodies send out their proper effluences to each other and to places about the earth. And it is upon these emanations from widely separated parts that the goetist seizes; he transmutes them by abnormally commingling their energies, perverts, misdirects, transfers, and concentrates them to a purpose different from that for which they were imparted (IV, 8). It is evident, therefore, that in this shifting of balance 'parts are compressed and weighed down, though at the same time wholes remain impassive to a molestation of this kind' (IV, 9). Though Ariel is a rational being and possessed of a will safe from human compulsion, his substance is composed of a 'spiritual matter'—which enables him to participate in physical matter—and this substance is merely an organic part of the universe. Accord-

ingly, when Sycorax concentrated the involuntary effluxions from a large number of other universe-parts
upon his spiritual matter, she was enabled to com-
press it to the point of fixing it in a cloven pine. But
having so disordered the corporeal world, which instantly righted itself into a new balance, she could
not undo her charm. Consequently, Ariel must remain
in the tree until liberated by Prospero, the theurgist.

Prospero is evidently a theurgist of high rank. But
we cannot determine precisely the degree of his at-
tainments. It is clear, however, that his higher soul is
not yet completely assimilated to the gods because
he has not yet freed himself from all human passions
and from interest in personal affairs. Though his passions are apparently under control, he nevertheless
displays irritation with Miranda's lack of attention
and something like anger with Ariel's desire for freedom. He becomes so vexed with Caliban and the con-
spirators that he must walk to still his beating mind;
such a disturbance in his troubled brain he recognizes
as infirmity and weakness. We cannot claim for him,
therefore, that complete union with divinity in which
the theurgist becomes, like the gods, altogether impassive. His ability to command rational daemons,
however, proves beyond a doubt that he must energize in the sphere of at least ethereal daemons, whose
province in the natural order it is to govern rational
and through them irrational daemons. Thus identifying himself with this high order of daemons, he is able

188

to look upon the celestial realms and to view the gods with a clear understanding.[45] He is, therefore, only partially subject to Fate; he becomes in a measure prescient and is allotted the power of providentially attending to and correcting the evils which his brother and others have performed. And this consummation is achieved by virtue of the inexplicable theurgical symbols, furnished in the first place by the gods through the instrumentality of daemons and set down in his books of wisdom. What these symbols are precisely, it is impossible to say. But it is reasonable to suppose that they include images and characters, mystic paradigms of the world, names and numbers of animals in their relation to planets (V, 8), divine names in ancient languages (VII, 4), antique prayers and incantations (VII, 5), and other paraphernalia of ritualistic worship.[46] Here Prospero no doubt finds explicit directions for his employment of magic robe and staff, enchanted circles and airy charms. He does not understand these signs and symbols; they are significant only to the gods who established them. But when Prospero the theurgist thinks them, these inexplicable signs themselves perform their proper function of exciting the will of the gods, who recognize their own images. And his works of enchantment are made possible. Hence it is not surprising to find Caliban insisting upon the destruction of the enchanter's books as a necessary prologue to the conspiracy's success. Says he:

> . . . there mayst brain him,
> Having first seized his books . . .
>                     Remember
> First to possess his books; for without them
> He's but a sot, as I am, nor hath not
> One spirit to command . . .
>                 Burn but his books.

And Prospero himself, when he determines to abjure theurgical practices, signifies that the source of his power lies in the book which he proposes to drown.

But the application of Prospero's power is necessarily made, according to the constitution of nature, through the instrumentality of daemons. We must remember that all the processes of nature are under the immediate supervision of specially appointed daemons of various ranks. And the theurgist must always employ the established machinery. That Ariel, Prospero's chief minister, is of aerial rank and therefore a rational being, cannot be doubted. It is significant that throughout the drama he is allowed to exercise largely his own judgment in the execution of his master's commands. In general the enchanter orders results, and the minister produces them by self-chosen methods and through the instrumentality of natural forces which he himself controls. For example, if a tempest is desired which may seem to confound Prospero's enemies but which in reality places them safely in his power, Ariel conducts the progress of it with gusto and with independent initiative. He raises such a coil of roaring waters that sky and sea seem to meet; his *phasmata,* or natural luminous appearances, flame such amazement upon the King's ship—now on the beak, now in the waist, the deck, in every cabin—that the mariners quit the vessel. All those aboard the apparently doomed ship, however, he lands safely and disperses them about the island; he chooses an odd angle of the island upon which to land Ferdinand, elects to hide the undamaged vessel in a certain deep nook known to both master and servant, charms the mariners to sleep and leaves them safely stowed under hatches. In like manner almost all of Prospero's enchantments are performed under the direction of that rational creature, Ariel.

Though some of the master's commands are executed by Ariel alone, in the performance of others he is aided by lesser ministers. This is precisely as it should be; for these meaner powers must be identified with aquatic, terrestrial and subterranean daemons —all irrational creatures—over which, in the order of nature, Ariel as rational being normally has supervision. For instance, at one point these lesser ministers appear as strange Shapes, bringing in and taking out a banquet before Prospero's enemies; Ariel plays the part of a harpy. Prospero approves of this quaint device:

> Bravely the figure of this harpy hast thou
> Perform'd, my Ariel; a grace it had devouring . . .
> so, with good life

And observation strange, my meaner ministers
Their several kinds have done (III, iii, 83 ff.).

Again, in the masque presented for the entertainment
of Miranda and Ferdinand, Ariel plays the part of
Ceres and no doubt directs the whole action; but the
rôles of Iris, Juno, Reapers, and Nymphs are sustained by the meaner spirits. Elsewhere, Trinculo,
Stephano, and Caliban are hunted by minor Spirits
in the shapes of dogs and hounds, with Prospero and
Ariel setting them on. And Prospero controls his
servant Caliban through the instrumentality of daemons in the form of firebrands, apes, hedgehogs, and
adders. Indeed, all of the enchanter's enemies are
finally brought into his presence for judgment and the
injustice which they have done is righted by means
of daemonic powers over which the theurgist has
gained control.

As one might expect, moreover, Prospero's instruments are represented as being ministers of Fate, or
its equivalent, Destiny. In the economy of the universe, as we have seen, the higher kingdom which
rules over both intellectuals and sensibles is called
the realm of Providence; and the subordinate kingdom which controls the world of created things alone
is the realm of Fate. Accordingly, Ariel recognizes
Destiny as the power which 'hath to instrument this
lower world and what is in it,' *i.e.*, 'that single unitary world-nature which creates, relates, and moves
all material bodies.' And since all nature is under

the guardianship of daemons, Ariel cannot be wrong when he says: 'I and my fellows Are the ministers of Fate' (III, iii, 53). As such these divine natures are invulnerable, though Ariel himself is subject to pain, pleasure, and a semblance of tender affections. At any rate, as ministers of Fate one of their duties is to inform men what ought not to be done and from what it is fitting to abstain. As Iamblichus says:

> They also give assistance to just works, but impede such as are unjust; and as many endeavour to take away unjustly the property of others, or basely to injure or destroy some one, they cause these to suffer the same things as they have done to others (IV, 1).

Exercising his proper function, therefore, Ariel pronounces a conditional curse upon Prospero's enemies:

> But remember—
> For that's my business to you—that you three
> From Milan did supplant good Prospero;
> Exposed unto the sea, which hath requit it,
> Him and his innocent child: for which foul deed
> The powers, delaying, not forgetting, have
> Incensed the seas and shores, yea, all the creatures,
> Against your peace. Thee of thy son, Alonso,
> They have bereft; and do pronounce by me
> Lingering perdition, worse than any death
> Can be at once, shall step by step attend
> You and your ways (III, iii, 70 ff.).

Thus the intellectual souls of these wicked men have been drowned, as it were, in evil passions; they are caught in the web of Fate, from which there is no escape except through repentance and complete restitution, through 'heart-sorrow and a clear life ensuing.'

Prospero recognizes his ministers and acknowledges their indispensable assistance in the performance of his theurgical operations. Following Golding's translation of Ovid's *Metamorphoses,* he identifies the irrational daemons of the Neo-Platonic system with the fairy creatures of English folk-mythology. He indicates that his 'weak masters' are the 'elves of hills, brooks, standing lakes and groves,' nymphs 'that on the sand with printless foot Do chase the ebbing Neptune and to fly him when he comes back,' and 'demi-puppets' or fairies that by moonshine make green sour ringlets and midnight mushrooms (V, i, 34 ff.). Such an assimilation of the creatures of folk-belief into the ranks of sublunary daemons is already common in the Renaissance. Robert Kirk, for example, says that 'Fairies . . . are said to be of a middle Nature betuixt Man and Angel, as were Daemons thought to be of old.' [47] Regarding the origin of fairies, the author of *A Discourse Concerning Devils and Spirits* likewise observes: 'The Platonists affirm that their nature is middle between Heaven and Hell; and that they reign in a third Kingdom from both, having no other judgment or doom to expect forever.' [48] The same author, after characterizing aerial daemons, says:

Subordinate unto these of the Air are the Terrestrial Spirits, which are of several degrees according to the places which they occupy, as Woods, Mountains, Caves, Fens, Mines, Ruins, Desolate places, and Ancient Buildings, called by the Antient Heathens after various names, as Nymphs, Satyrs, Lamii, Dryades, Sylvanes, Cobali, &c. And more particularly the Faeries, who do principally inhabit the Mountains, and Caverns of the earth.[49]

It is very fitting, therefore, that Prospero should address his meaner ministers as demi-puppets: they may be considered as *puppets* in the sense that they are subject to his will; and they are called *demi*-puppets because, in the order of nature, they are the mediators between man and the gods, or 'of a middle Nature betuixt Man and Angels,' or (if one cares to use Christian phraseology) because 'their nature is middle between Heaven and Hell.'[50] With the aid, then, of terrestrial spirits, *i.e.,* aquatic, terrestrial, and subterranean daemons, Prospero the theurgist has performed his enchantments. Commanding Ariel, who controls these irrational servants, he has made it appear as if the noonday sun were dimmed, has called forth the mutinous winds, given fire to the rattling thunder and rifted Jove's stout oak with his own bolt; he has been able to initiate earthquakes and to call forth the spirits of the dead from their graves.

All of Prospero's enchantments in *The Tempest*, however, are to be considered in the end as but a 'rough magic.' He determines to abjure it; he'll break his staff and bury it certain fathoms in the earth, and deeper than did ever plummet sound he'll drown his book. Why? The answer is not far to seek. Theurgical practices, as we have seen, represent no more than a means of preparation for the intellectual soul in its upward progress; union with the intelligible gods is the theurgist's ultimate aim. Prospero has used his powers benevolently in the righting of wrongs, and in the process his soul is cleansed of its baser passions. His nobler reason taking part now against his fury, he finds that the rarer action is in virtue than in vengeance. He forgives the rankest faults of his enemies—demanding, however, strict justice in restitution—and so finds himself at the close of the play immeasurably nearer than before to the impassivity of the gods. His theurgical operations have accomplished their purpose.[51] He wishes now to take the final step and to consummate the assimilation of his soul to the gods. And this step is to be accomplished through prayer. Says he:

> Now I want
> Spirits to enforce, art to enchant,
> And my ending is despair,
> Unless I be relieved by prayer,
> Which pierces so that it assaults
> Mercy itself and frees all faults (Epilogue).

Here is no suggestion of outward ritual; 'true prayer for the Neo-Platonist is an inward tension of the will.' [52] And prayer, according to Plotinus, 'attains its effect by a community of feeling betwixt certain parts of the universe, which lie as it were along the same stretched cord, so that if the cord be twitched at its lower extremity the tremor is felt above.' [53] Before we can experience the ultimate mysteries, therefore, we must 'ask help of God himself, not in public speech, but in prayer within the soul extending ourselves toward him; for praying thus we can be alone with God.' [54] And it is worth repeating that we are able to extend ourselves toward him because, as Iamblichus says,

We preserve in the soul collectively the mystic and arcane image of the Gods, and through this we elevate the soul to the Gods, and when elevated conjoin it as much as possible with them (VII, 4).

Understanding these principles, Prospero would now engage in that prayer which frees from all faults and fits man to be alone with the gods. Thus he still adheres to theurgical principles in attempting to achieve the utmost reach of which the human soul is capable.

After this manner, it seems to me, Shakespeare has employed concepts of sacerdotal science as the philosophical pattern of *The Tempest*. A theurgical system complete in all its ramifications is, of course, not exhibited in this drama; the artist is not interested primarily in the popular Neo-Platonic philosophy as such. For purely artistic purposes he has chosen only dramatically appropriate elements of theurgical science, but these selections may reasonably imply his acquaintance with the whole system. Accordingly it has seemed necessary, if we are to understand what he has used, to sketch in some detail the essential and pertinent background of Neo-Platonic opinion on these matters: the origin, structure, and operation of the universe, with special reference to nature, together with the essence and powers of the human creature and his relations to whatever forces there are about him. That is to say, though our main purpose has been to define and reveal in operation a set of relationships, we have found it necessary to determine the essence of the terms related. It must be observed, moreover, that we have not been greatly concerned with the concrete expressions of either legitimate or illegitimate magic; the sources of these dramatic instances may be safely left to the investigations of exponents of comparative literature.[55] This study does attempt to reconstruct the rationale of those powers which are capable of producing such magic effects in a universe of given texture. We cannot escape the conclusion, therefore, that Shakespeare is here undertaking what he supposes to be classical drama. The philosophical pattern of his *Macbeth,* as has been shown elsewhere, is mediaeval, scholastic, and Christian.[56] But in *The Tempest,* with its Neo-Platonic concepts serving as artistic pattern and with its unities of time and place, the artist is revealed as having passed definitely under the influence of Renaissance thought. He no longer employs Christian myth as the integrating principle of tragedy; here he creates an altogether different world, which is dominated by classical myth and integrated by a purely pagan philosophy.[57] This must not be interpreted to mean that Shakespeare's own philosophy has been altered from Christian to pagan; his personal philosophy cannot be determined from a study of his dramas. It does signify that he is always the objective and versatile artist, who is willing to select any philosophical concept appropriate to his purposes and to utilize it as the formative principle of his drama.[58]

199

# APPENDIX A: *PATTERNS*

## Appendix A

## PATTERNS

### I

MODERN Aesthetics attempts to define processes of creation in the mind of an artist and to show that the creative act is 'intuitive expression.' The internal work of art, or aesthetic fact, is said to be a spontaneous and free product of the contemplative consciousness and as such cannot be circumscribed by a fiat of the will. Since the consciousness which accompanies its production is contemplative and in no sense reflective, the internal work of art would seem to be independent of time and space, of unreality and reality, and completely indifferent to moral and practical considerations. The artist presumably entertains no purpose in submitting himself to the creating of it, and he expects it to have no force in the realm of utility.[1]

Externalized art, on the other hand, is the product of both contemplative and deliberative consciousness. It involves an exercise of will; it embodies an expression of purpose, and a consideration of the practical ends of communication. This artistic fact is a sort of

203

symbol, or organic construction in the phenomenal
world, in which the deliberating artist attempts to fix
for himself and for us such aspects of his vision as
will suggest to our creative imaginations the whole
of his intuitive experience. Interpretation of such
art-works of the past must always be difficult because
these artistic facts have arisen in situations and under circumstances quite at variance with those familiar to us. Production may have involved both a form
and content in a measure foreign to our experience.
It becomes necessary, therefore, for us to recreate
historically the age which generated the work of art
before we can understand its symbolism. Such re-
integration of the psychological and historical conditions from which the art-work emerged, we may suppose, is one function of the scholar. It is conceivable
that he may profitably direct his attention to the artistic pattern alone.

II

Now, an artistic pattern may be defined as any
form or contour in accordance with which the artist
fixes in an external art object the selected and fused
materials of his vision. No one must suppose it to be,
mechanically speaking, a sort of mold into which
transformed life-materials are flowed. It is rather an
active, formative principle which, combining in some

204

mysterious manner with the stuff of art, determines not only the shape of the externalized product but also in some measure the quality and nature of its content. This must be carefully distinguished from the aesthetic pattern, *i.e., form,* which combines actively with *content* in the production of the aesthetic fact.[2] The aesthetic pattern cannot be thought of as having an existence independent of the content which it elaborates. The artistic pattern, on the other hand, is a concept, and as such it may have enjoyed for a long time an autonomous existence in the realm of knowledge. When, however, the artist deliberately chooses it as the formative principle of his externalized work, it must surrender its independence and, without completely losing its identity as a concept, subordinate itself to the artistic whole. In proportion as its conceptual vitality tends to dominate the finished product, the result is not an artistic but a scientific work. But when the artistic pattern exercises its function successfully, it seems to melt into the artistic fact so unobtrusively that one is likely to ignore its identity or at least to be only dimly conscious of its activity. Still the pattern may be disengaged from the externalized work of art and examined. Warning must be given, however, that the pattern disengaged may appear warped when compared with the same pattern serving as the formative principle of the work of art, because pattern and content exercise a reciprocally transforming influence the one upon the other. And one pattern is likely to be affected in some measure by other patterns in the same work.

Poetic drama, for example, is likely to embody a greater variety of patterns—or since it is an artistically unified whole, a more complicated pattern-system—than possibly any other kind of art. Considered as a poem alone, it will illustrate the fact that dramatic content has been fixed in a very definite *metrical pattern,* such as iambic pentameter, rimed or unrimed. Except in the case of purely mechanical verse, however, such a pattern is to be considered merely as a norm, from which the poet varies within limits in order that he may attain a greater flexibility of line and, consequently, a wider freedom in the expression of thought and emotion. A dramatist's selection of the poetic form in dramatic representation is not an arbitrary matter; it is not as if poetry were merely an added ornament which may be employed or not. Since poetry is the natural language of the emotions, the dramatist finds it a fundamental necessity in the adequate presentation of situations involving emotional upheavals of any sort. He does not, therefore, emphasize the metrical pattern but subordinates it to the more fundamental *rhythmic patterns,* which are created out of groups of flexible lines or part-lines and which clothe precisely the rhythmic rise and fall of the emotional content. Though one may still be conscious of the more or less regular beat of the metrical feet, attention is compelled primarily to the rhythmic patterns, to the musical phrasing, as it were, which gives to any passage its peculiarly dramatic quality. And fused with these interweaving and supporting patterns is discernible what may be called the *image-pattern, i.e.,* the unique expression of the poetic imagination in words, which stimulates our imaginations to grasp the dramatic content. This is also absorbed into the rhythmic pattern and becomes an important part of the whole, namely, dramatic poetry.

In externalizing his inner work of art, moreover, the mind of the dramatic artist necessarily passes from the aesthetic to the logical [3] in order that he may show the proper relations between the artistic facts which he presents. He may attempt to harmonize the incidents of his plot by reducing them to a strict chronological order; indeed, whatever other relations exist between such facts, they seem to occur in a definite time-sequence. This is the *chronological pattern.* In the arrangement of content-elements the artist may also give special attention to the production of a certain tonal effect which surrounds and pervades the action. This is the *atmosphere pattern.* Or he is likely to achieve the greatest unity by representing a series of actions or incidents causally connected —in the sense that one logically begets another or that all together produce in this manner a given result

—leading inevitably, if it is a tragic drama, to an end called the catastrophe. Greek tragedy, with its main emphasis upon plot and its logical ordering of fable-elements into the Aristotelian beginning, middle, and end, illustrates this type of integration admirably. This is called the *logical pattern*. When scrutinized objectively the bare plot of any well-constructed drama seems to grow in some sort after this fashion. But it does not follow that any logical sequence of external actions constitutes dramatic action.

Modern drama complicates and expands the logical pattern immensely by subsuming under it the psychological reactions of the characters involved. Psychology attempts to reduce the spiritual life of man to schemes or types,[4] and almost any drama since the sixteenth century is likely to reflect in some measure the current psychological tenets. For example, a dramatic character created during the Renaissance may be expected to function in accordance with doctrines of the old faculty psychology; a twentieth-century character, on the other hand, may react in conformity with Freudian, or behavioristic, or associational principles. But whatever the scheme may be, a dramatic character should be consistent and in harmony with himself throughout the drama. This is the *psychological pattern*. But a series of incidents or episodes logically arranged is not in itself dramatic; feeling or emotion or an exercise of will, however moving, is not in itself dramatic.[5] In a great drama one may expect to find a certain complex interrelation between emotion and will, on the one hand, and incidents or deeds, on the other. The unity of dramatic action, in a modern drama especially, is apt to depend upon the spiritual integrity, the continuity of emotional processes, and the logical ordering and steeling of the will of the chief character or characters. Since the age of Shakespeare we have come to recognize that the act as represented in the bare fable is of importance only as it reveals or further affects the underlying spiritual, mental, and emotional processes. Deeds which, when woven together, seem to form a plot, but which may be merely episodic and on the surface entirely disconnected one from the other and from the incident of the catastrophe, become straightway significant when they are seen in their proper aspects as expressions or originators of continuous inner activities. Such a logical arrangement of plot and character elements may be called the *logico-psychological pattern*. Occasionally this dramatic action, as such complete in itself and self-sufficient, can be interpreted as the symbolical representation of an ulterior action, which may or may not contribute by way of universality to the drama. This is the *allegorical pattern*.

But in tragic drama the all-integrating and absorbing principle is the *philosophical pattern*. The province of general philosophy, we may suppose, is to furnish a rational account of man's nature and his place in the universe. Its conclusions are based upon the findings of all the other natural, mental, and moral sciences. It fashions concepts covering all reality—the active and passive character of nature, the laws which seem to govern vital and created forces, the function and ultimate end of man. In a word, it locates man in relation to all the mysteries which surround him. Now the dramatic artist is rarely, if ever, a philosopher in the sense that he builds a philosophical system of his own. Like the rest of us, he most probably evolves his *Weltanschauung* from an examination of principles found in systematic philosophy. But whether his philosophical thinking is original or not, when he comes to communicate his aesthetic experience, he is always primarily the creative artist and not the philosopher. There is no reason, however, why he should not appropriate any philosophical concept at hand and utilize it as the formative principle of his work of art. For example, an Ibsen may conceive of his characters as fundamentally social creatures, produced and governed in all their actions by natural forces, mainly heredity and environment. An Aeschylus, on the other hand, may conceive of man as a free, moral being whose every act comes under the immediate judgment of the gods. In the tragic destiny of an Aeschylean character, therefore, one must recognize the working out of two principles: namely, transgression against the divine will brings inevitable suffering and death, and the just gods visit sins of fathers upon the children to the third and fourth generations. In either case the drama is achieved under the formative influence of a philosophical concept.

### III

This philosophical pattern must be carefully distinguished from philosophical content. In a tragic drama almost any character is likely to attempt a rationalization of his experience in relation to the causal forces about him; he may even suggest a complete philosophical system. But it is his own, and may have little or nothing to do with the integrating principle which the artist employs. As Croce aptly remarks: 'He who conceives a tragedy puts into a crucible a great quantity, so to say, of impressions: expressions themselves, conceived on other occasions, are fused with the new in a single mass, in the same way as we can cast into a melting furnace formless pieces of bronze and choicest statuettes. Those choicest statuettes must be melted just like the pieces of bronze, before there can be a new statue.' [6] Thus the philosophical concepts in a drama, if they are properly fused, no longer stand as such independently; they may have become simply elements of characterization. In proportion, therefore, as the dramatist's main purpose is to express his own philosophical system through the medium of his *dramatis per-*

*sonae,* he becomes less the artist and more the pure scientist. It is true that occasionally the maxims put into the mouths of characters may represent the author's point of view for the time being, but that fact is relevant only as it indicates to what degree he is imaginatively absorbed into the person speaking. Or even if such concepts should chance to coincide with the dramatist's own world-view, this fact will not be readily discovered; the true artist always subordinates his own personality to that of the dramatic character. Attempting, therefore, to reconstruct an author's point of view from the philosophical content of a drama is a futile procedure.

If the dramatic artist has a philosophy of his own, one is more likely to compass it through a study of his philosophical patterns. Here one might discover some inkling of his conceptions regarding the human actors he represents and the ultimate causes which impel their happiness or destruction. But even so, we must not rashly conclude that these conceptions are part and parcel of his personal belief, or faith, or general philosophy. They may be such, but not necessarily so. Indeed the wise artist does well to avoid employing his own philosophy as a formative principle in his dramatic creations, because by doing so he escapes a manifold danger. In the first place, a man's personal philosophy is to him so vivid and comprehensive, so warm by reason of his conception of eternal values, that he is apt to turn prophet and campaign actively for the spread of his gospel. Danger now grows heavy that his primary purpose will become, not to communicate an aesthetic experience, but to preach his doctrines by subordinating dramatic content to the demands of his philosophical pattern. The result of such emphasis is a thesis play and not a work of art. Or if, being a super-artist, he may succeed in utilizing his own philosophy as the integrating principle of a single work, he is not justified in attempting to employ it in a series of dramas; violating the integrity of dramatic materials that are essentially diverse by wrenching them always into the same philosophical mold leads to intolerable monotony. This suggests a more essential distinction: it is to be doubted whether those principles which shape the artist's character and form the contour of his life in relation to the mysteries about him are ever precisely adapted for use in the realm of his drama. A tragic drama is not life; its action, in some sense an imitation of life, moves nevertheless in a world separate and distinct from that in which the artist lives and from that of all other dramas. That is to say, the ultimate success of a tragedy depends largely upon the degree to which its action is objectified and confined within its own limits. We may conclude, therefore, that the dramatic artist is, in his philosophical activities, always eclectic; from various sources he chooses the thought and opinion which seem to him best adapted to his artistic purposes in a specific case, fuses them—colored, of course, by his personality—into philosophical content, or involves them as philosophical pattern.

Research in the field of dramatic patterns must always be perplexing and in its results never completely satisfactory. When we consider the bewildering variety of patterns constituting the artistic form of a drama, and understand how as active principles they work harmoniously together, complementing and supporting one another, intermingling, and shaping content into a perfect unity, difficulties in the way of interpreting them as a whole or of isolating a single pattern for examination would seem to be almost insurmountable. Yet scholarship busies itself continually with the investigation of patterns, their origin, historical development, and function in particular dramas. For example, any interpreter may, according to the dictates of his taste or momentary inclination, center his attention exclusively upon the metrical form of the work in question, or upon the plot elements in their temporal or logical relationships; he may consider only the psychological motivation of characters or the philosophical patterns. He must not suppose, however, that his metrical studies represent adequately the poetry itself of the drama or that his analysis of the psychological motivation can accomplish more than merely suggest the living characters. Nor may his conclusions regarding one or more of the patterns be recognized as an interpretation of the work as a whole. But within proper limits such investigations are extremely profitable; they furnish a basis for illuminating syntheses and for creative criticism.

APPENDIX B: *NOTES*

## Appendix B

## Notes to Chapter I

[1] *The Epithalamium of Petrus Aegidius*, trans. N. Bailey, ed. E. Johnson, London, 1878, I, 384; *The Epistles of Erasmus*, ed. F. M. Nichols, New York, 1901, I, 144; II, 22.

[2] *The Praise of Folly*, quoted at some length by A. R. Pennington, *The Life and Character of Erasmus*, London, 1875, pp. 84–89.

[3] *Antibarbarorum liber*, ed. Albert Hyma in *The Youth of Erasmus*, Ann Arbor, 1930, pp. 242–331; see pp. 199, 203. Cf. E. Emerton, *Desiderius Erasmus of Rotterdam*, New York, 1899, p. 72.

[4] Such as Lorenzo Valla; see Hyma, *op. cit.*, pp. 10, 187, 189.

[5] *Op. cit.*, p. 199.

[6] See Arthur C. McGiffert, *Martin Luther: The Man and His Work*, New York, 1912, pp. 15, 34; Preserved Smith, *The Life and Letters of Martin Luther*, New York, 1911, pp. 5–6, 12, 13, 59.

[7] See Smith, *op. cit.*, p. 24.

[8] McGiffert, *op. cit.*, pp. 62–63.

[9] Fr. Eby, *Early Protestant Educators*, New York, 1931, pp. 35–37; cf. Smith, *op. cit.*, p. 185; McGiffert, *op. cit.*, p. 63.

[10] Cf. McGiffert, *op. cit.*, p. 63.

[11] *The Advancement of Learning*, ed. Joseph Davy, London, 1904, Bk. I (Bohn, p. 43).

[12] *Ibid.*, pp. 46–47.

[13] *Ibid.*, p. 45.

[14] Cf. Thomas Fowler, in Introduction to his edition of *Novum Organum*, Oxford, 1878, p. 15.

[15] *Novum Organum*, I, 116; *The Advancement of Learning*, p. 47.

[16] Maurice De Wulf, *History of Mediaeval Philosophy*, trans. E. C. Messenger, New York, 1926, I, 1–3; II, 265 ff. (I have not yet had access to the 2nd. Ed. of Vol. I.)

[17] *Ibid.*, I, 3–4.

[18] *Op. cit.*, p. 5.

[19] W. H. Hudson, *The Story of the Renaissance*, New York, 1924, pp. 131–132.

[20] See Walter Pater, *The Renaissance*, New York, 1908, pp. 51 ff.;

John Addington Symonds, *Renaissance in Italy*, New York, 1883, p. 333.

21 Quoted from Symonds, *op. cit.*, p. 334.

22 On the decline of scholasticism and the persistence of various schools through the sixteenth century, see De Wulf, *op. cit.*, II, 287–291 (Nominalism), 291–300 (Realism), 315–316; W. Windelband, *A History of Philosophy*, trans. James H. Tufts, New York, 1931, pp. 352–377. (Quotations from Windelband in this chapter are made by permission of The Macmillan Co., publishers.)

23 See Windelband, *op. cit.*, 352 ff.

24 *Ibid.*, p. 353, 363, on the Council of Trent, 1563.

25 *Ibid.*, p. 363.

26 Lily B. Campbell, *Shakespeare's Tragic Heroes: Slaves of Passion*, Cambridge, 1930, pp. 47 ff.

27 *Op. cit.*, p. 383.

28 *Op. cit.*, II, 316.

29 Quoted from Symonds, *op. cit.*, pp. 48–49.

30 On the mediaeval emphasis upon man as a microcosm, see De Wulf, *op. cit.*, I, 137, 214, 229, 301, 312, 330; II, 248; and on the Renaissance employment of the idea, Windelband, *op. cit.*, pp. 366 ff.; Campbell, *op. cit.*, pp. 50–62; Ruth Leila Anderson, *Elizabethan Psychology and Shakespeare's Plays*, Iowa City, 1927, pp. 61 ff., etc.

31 Quoted from Pater, *op. cit.*, p. 42.

32 De Wulf, *op. cit.*, II, 316.

33 *Of the Laws of Ecclesiastical Polity*, ed. Isaac Walton, Oxford, 1807, I. References within parentheses in the text are to pages of this edition and volume.

34 Compare Thomas Aquinas, *Summa Theologica*, I. 11. 1–4; I. 14. 8; Windelband, *op. cit.*, pp. 251–255.

35 Cf. Thomas, I–II. 93. 1.

36 *Ibid.*, I. 115. 2. c; De Wulf, *op. cit.*, I, 118 ff.

37 Cf. Thomas, I–II. 90.

38 Thomas discusses at length both concepts, I–II. 91, 93.

39 Cf. Thomas, I–II. 94.

40 Cf. Thomas, I–II. 96, 97.

41 Cf. *ibid.*, I. 106–114 for angelology and demonology.

42 Cf. Thomas, I–II. 91. 2.

43 Cf. *ibid.*, I–II. 94. 1.

44 On the universal adoption by scholasticism of this central theory of Aristotelianism, see De Wulf, *op. cit.*, I, 277 ff. But, says he, "It is important to note that the scholastics extend the theory of potency and act far beyond the limits in which Aristotle confined it. They apply it to all contingent beings, corporeal and incorporeal, and in corporeal

being itself, to realms undreampt of by the Stagirite," I, 277. So does
Hooker.

45 Cf. De Wulf, *op. cit.*, I, 293–95.

46 *Ibid.*, pp. 295–96.

47 *Ibid.*, pp. 297–98; Thomas, I, 5. 1, 3; I–II, 18, 1, etc.

48 De Wulf, *op. cit.*, I, 298; Windelband, *op. cit.*, pp. 328–37;
Thomas, I. 79. 1–8; I. 83. 4; I–II. 77. 1; I–II. 80. 2. Here Hooker has
evidently adopted the Thomist conception of psychological determinism.

49 Such men as Hugo Grotius and Sir Thomas More also depended
upon the mediaeval conception of Natural Law and its corollaries in
their statement of the natural and social rights of man; see De Wulf,
*op. cit.*, II, 279.

50 *Op. cit.*, II, 316.

51 See Mr. Allen Tate, "New England Culture and Emily Dickinson,"
*The Symposium*, April, 1932, p. 222.

52 Viola B. Hulbert, *Spenser's Twelve Moral Virtues "According to
Aristotle and the Rest,"* in University of Chicago *Abstracts of Theses*,
Humanistic Series, V, 479–485.

53 See Hardin Craig, "The Ethics of *King Lear*," *PQ.*, IV (1925),
97 ff.; Campbell, *op. cit.*, *passim*.

54 Hardin Craig, "Shakespeare's Depiction of Passions," *PQ.*, IV,
301. Cf. Anderson, *op. cit.*, *passim;* Mary Isabelle O'Sullivan, *PMLA.*,
XLI (1926) 667–679; Murray W. Bundy, *JEPh.*, XXIII (1924),
516–549.

55 Quoted and paraphrased from De Wulf, *Philosophy and Civilization in the Middle Ages*, Princeton University Press, 1922, p. 176,
note 28. (By permission of the publishers.)


# NOTES TO CHAPTER II

1 For these readings and interpretations, see Furness, Variorum
Shakespeare, *Macbeth*, IV, i, 64.

2 Hardin Craig, *Shakespeare*, 1931, p. 921, note 59. The *N. E. D.*, s.v.
*germen*, says, 'The rudiment of an organism, a germ.'

3 This exposition is taken from Dr. E. Zeller's *The Stoics, Epicureans, and Sceptics*, trans. O. J. Reichel, New York, 1892, pp. 165–73.

4 See Davidson, *The Stoic Creed*, p. 88; *The Meditations*, of Marcus
Aurelius, trans. A. I. Trannoy, Paris, 1925, 9. 1.

5 Based on William Ralph Inge, *The Philosophy of Plotinus*, London,
1929, I, 155 ff.

6 Plotinus, *Opera Omnia*, ed. Fr. Creuzer and G. H. Moser (with

Commentaries and Interpretations of Marsilius Ficinus), Oxford, 1835, I, 264 (*Enneads*, 2. 3. 17). I quote from *Plotinus' Complete Works*, trans. K. S. Guthrie, London, p. 1196.

7 This exposition is based on Maurice De Wulf, *The History of Mediaeval Philosophy*, trans. E. C. Messenger, New York, 1926, I, 118 ff.

8 Cf. St. Augustine, *De Genesi ad Literam*, Lib. VIII, xxviii, in *Opera Omnia, Castigata*, etc. Monachorum Ordinis Sancti Benedicti, Parisiis, 1837, III, 365.

9 *De Trinitate*, III, viii, 3 (*loc. cit.*, VIII, col. 1229); I use the translation of A. W. Haddon, *The Nicene and Post-Nicene Fathers*, First Ser., III, 60 ff.

10 *De Divinitatis Essentia Monologium*, cap. IX, Migne *Patr. Lat.*, 158, *Opera Omnia*, col. 157.

11 *Ibid.*, cap. XIII, col. 161.

12 De Wulf, *op. cit.*, I, 366.

13 *Ibid.*, I, 392. De Wulf quotes from a letter published by Ehrle, *Der Augustinismus*, etc., in *Archiv. Litter. und Kirchengesch. Mittelalters*, V (1889), 620, 623, to which I have not had access.

14 Quoted from De Wulf, *op. cit.*, II, 42.

15 *Ibid.*, I, 401, 402.

16 *Opus Tertium*, ed. J. S. Brewer, Rolls Series (1859), p. 127. See also pp. 122–129, *passim*.

17 De Wulf, *op. cit.*, II, 139.

18 See *ibid.*, II, 18.

19 *Summa Theologica*, I. 115. 2. c. I use in the text translations of the *Summa* made by Fathers of the English Dominican Province, London, 1920 ff.

20 *Ibid.*

21 *Ibid.*, I. 115. 2, *ad* 1. De Wulf says that Duns Scotus also rejects the Augustinian doctrine of the seminal reasons *ad vitandam creationem aut annihilationem* (Rep. lib. II, dist. 18), but that he gives to the term *rationes seminales*, a restricted and special sense, *op. cit.*, II, 80, n. 5.

22 See Lynn Thorndike, *The History of Magic and Experimental Science*, II, 970 ff.

23 Iamblichus, *The Mysteries of the Egyptians, Chaldeans, and Assyrians*, trans. Thomas Taylor (the Platonist), London, 1895, p. 192. Taylor quotes a like passage from Simplicius's Commentary on the first book of Aristotle's *Physics:* 'Those things, indeed, which are the properties of sensibles are irrational, corporeal, distributed into parts, and passing into bulk and divulsion, through an ultimate progression into generation, viz., into matter. . . . And matter is, as it were, the receptacle of generated and sensible natures,' p. 361.

24 See Plotinus, Creuzer ed., I, 239.

25 *De Occulta Philosophia*, trans. into English, 1651, ed. Willis F. Whitehead, *Three Books of Occult Philosophy or Magic*, New York, 1897, Bk. I., ch. xci (p. 62).

26 *The Advancement of Learning*, Bk. III, ch. v.

27 *Novum Organum*, ed. Thomas Fowler, lib. I, cap. cxxi.

28 Thomas Norton, *The Ordinall of Alchimy*, reproduced in facsimile from Elias Ashmole's *Theatrum Chemicum Britannicum*, with introduction by E. J. Holmyard, Baltimore, 1931, p. 115. Cf. *ibid.*, pp. 116–117 and a curious passage in Sir Thomas Browne's *Religio Medici*, Sects. XXXI–XXXII.

29 *De Trinitate*, III, cap. 8.

30 *Ibid.*, III, 8–9 (Haddon, III, 60–63).

31 *Summa Theologica*, I. 110. 4, *ad* 3. Cf. I. 51. 3, *ad*. 5.

32 *Ibid.*, I. 114. 4, *ad* 2. He goes on to show, however, how such operations may be made to seem the work of demons.

33 *Ibid.*, I. 115. 2, *ad* 2. (Sir Thomas Browne echoes this doctrine: 'I conceive there is a traditional magick, not learned from the devil, but at second hand from his scholars, who, having once the secret betrayed, are able and do empirically practise without his advice; they both proceeding upon the principles of nature; where actives, aptly conjoined to disposed passives, will, under any master, produce their effects,' *op. cit.*, sect. XXXI.)

34 *Ibid.*, I. 115. 2, *ad* 4.

35 *Ibid.*, I. 110. 4, *ad* 2; I. 114. 5, *ad* 3, quoting from Augustine. For an excellent history of compacts between witches or sorcerers and the devil, see G. L. Kittredge, *Witchcraft in Old and New England*, p. 239 ff., with bibliographies.

36 *Summa Theologica*, I. 64. 1. c. References within parentheses in the following passages of the text are to the *Summa Theologica*.

37 This chapter appeared first in the North Carolina *Studies in Philology*, XXIX (1932), 15–28.

## NOTES TO CHAPTER III

1 See Lilian Winstanley, *Macbeth, King Lear, and Contemporary History* (Cambridge, 1922), pp. 104–15; T. A. Spalding, *Elizabethan Demonology* (London, 1880), pp. 90 ff.; Howard Furness, Variorum *Macbeth*, notes on the witch-scenes; Margaret Lucy, *Shakespeare and the Supernatural* (Liverpool, 1906), pp. 11–16, Bibliography by William Jaggard; Edwin Wiley, *A Study of the Supernatural in Three Plays of Shakespeare*, University of California *Chronicle*, XV (1913),

No. 4, pp. 40–42; C. E. Whitmore, *The Supernatural in Tragedy* (Cambridge, 1915), pp. 255–56; Lily B. Campbell, *Shakespeare's Tragic Heroes, Slaves of Passion* (Cambridge, 1930), pp. 87–89; Mildred Tonge, "Black Magic and Miracles in *Macbeth*," *Journal Eng. Germ. Philol.*, XXXI (1932), 234–46; E. E. Stoll, *Shakespearean Studies* (New York, 1927), p. 228; Montague Summers, *The History of Witchcraft and Demonology* (London, 1926), pp. 289–90. Cf. G. L. Kittredge, *Witchcraft in Old and New England* (Cambridge, 1928), *passim;* King James I, *Demonologie*, ed. G. B. Harrison (London, 1924) (Bodley Head Quartos); Reginald Scot, *Discoverie of Witchcraft*, ed. with *A Discourse of Devils and Spirits*, B. Nicholson (London, 1886), *passim.*

[2] Charlotte Carmichael, *Academy*, 8 Feb., 1879; Furness, p. 9; A. H. Tolman, "Notes on *Macbeth*," *PMLA.*, XI (1896), 200–12, etc.

[3] A. C. Bradley, *Shakespearean Tragedy* (New York, 1922), p. 342; Tonge, *op. cit.*, p. 236, etc.

[4] Spalding, *op. cit.*, p. 93.

[5] Lucy, *op. cit.*, p. 16; Furness, p. 408.

[6] G. G. Gervinus, *Shakespeare Commentaries*, trans. F. E. Bunnett, 5th ed. (London, 1892), p. 592.

[7] A. W. Schlegel, Furness, p. 430.

[8] Frederick Boas, *Shakespeare and His Predecessors* (New York, 1902), p. 413.

[9] A. C. Bradley, *op. cit.*, p. 348.

[10] Wiley, *op. cit.*, p. 50.

[11] *Ibid.*, p. 48.

[12] G. Wilson Knight, *The Wheel of Fire* (London, 1930), p. 161.

[13] Stoll, *op. cit.*, p. 228.

[14] Franz Horn, Furness, p. 431.

[15] J. L. F. Flathe, Furness, p. 446.

[16] Whitmore, *op. cit.*, p. 256.

[17] See Furness, p. 453.

[18] Cf. Stoll, *op. cit.*, p. 237.

[19] *The Advancement of Learning*, Bk. III, ch. ii, ed. Joseph Devy (London, 1904), p. 122.

[20] *Op. cit.*, p. 453.

[21] See Chapter II above.

[22] E. K. Chambers, *The Mediaeval Stage*, II, 91, 147–48.

[23] *Op. cit.*, pp. 256, 263–66. Cf. Summers, *op. cit.*, pp. 276–312.

[24] Whitmore says: "Shakespeare avails himself of this universally held belief, and presents his Weird Sisters at first under the guise of witches. . . . The Sisters do not derive their might from any covenant with the powers of evil, but are themselves such powers, owing their sinister capacities only to themselves," *op. cit.*, p. 256.

25 Quoted from footnote to Robert Burton, *The Anatomy of Melancholy*, Part I, Sect. II, Mem. I, Subs. ii (Bohn ed., I, 205).

26 *Ibid.*, I, 206; Maximilian Rudwin, *The Devil in Legend and Literature* (Chicago, 1931), pp. 94–104; *The Talmud, Midrashim, and Kabbala*, trans. in Universal Classics Library, with Intro. by M. H. Harris (Washington, 1901), pp. 76, 182, 186.

27 Rudwin, *op. cit.*, p. 19; *The Works of Flavius Josephus*, trans. W. Whiston, *Antiquities*, lib. I, cap. iii (London, 1872), p. 32; *The Book of Enoch*, VI–VIII, ed. R. H. Charles, in *Apocrypha and Pseudepigrapha of the Old Testament*, II, 193–94, and notes; Lactantius, *The Divine Institutes*, II, c. xv, trans. W. Fletcher, *Ante-Nicene Christian Library*, I, 126–28; Justin Martyr, *The Second Apology*, trans. M. Dods, *Ante-Nicene Chris. Lib.*, p. 75 (see for a discussion of demonology in the early fathers, Bishop John Kaye, *Some Account of the Writings and Opinions of Justin Martyr* [London, 1855], pp. 201–10) ; Athenagoras, *Writings*, trans. in *Ante-Nicene Christian Library*, p. 407, etc.

28 Burton, *loc. cit.;* Rudwin, *op. cit.*, p. 23, etc.

29 Dean W. R. Inge, *The Philosophy of Plotinus* (London, 1929), II, 198; Burton, *loc. cit.;* Lynn Thorndike, *The History of Magic and Experimental Science* (New York, 1923), I, 204, etc.

30 Inge, *op. cit.*, II, 199; Thorndike, *op. cit.*, II, 55, 208, 227, 461.

31 See Apuleius, *The God of Socrates*, trans. in Bohn, pp. 350–73; K. Svoboda, *La Démonologie de Michel Psellos*, Brno, 1927; Scot, *op. cit.*, pp. 508–18; Thorndike *op. cit.*, II, 55, 104, 285, 317, 357; Iamblichus, *The Mysteries of the Egyptians*, trans. Thomas Taylor (London, 1895), pp. 78, 82, 97–98, 160, 198, 220–23, 313 ff., 340, 364; Plotinus, *Opera omnia*, ed. Fred. Creuzer (Oxonii, 1835) ; see Index for Plotinus' conception of daemons and for Ficinus's commentaries; Inge, *op. cit.*, II, 197 ff.

32 Rudwin, *op. cit.*, p. 21 ff.

33 *Ibid.*, p. 22; Minor White Latham, *The Elizabethan Fairies* (New York, 1930), pp. 23–64.

34 Rudwin, *op. cit.*, pp. 5–8; King James, *op. cit.*, Bk. I, cap. vi; Scot, *op. cit.*, pp. 421 ff.

35 *Op. cit.*, I, 214.

36 See Christian D. Ginsburg, *The Kabbalah* (1925), pp. 83–114.

37 Iamblichus, *op. cit.*, pp. 220–21, 343–47; on the theurgy of Porphyry, Iamblichus, and Proclus, see W. Windelband, *A History of Philosophy*, trans. J. H. Tufts (New York, 1931), p. 250. On magic see Thorndike, *op. cit.*, *passim;* Martino del Rio, *Disquisitionum magicarum libri sex* (Lvgdvni, 1608), *passim;* Scot, *op. cit.*, Appendix, I, pp. 471–91; H. Littledale, "Folklore and Superstitions:

Ghosts and Fairies; Witchcraft and Devils," in *Shakespeare's England* (Oxford, 1926), I, 516 ff.

38 Windelband, *op. cit.*, p. 247; see also pp. 244–51. Cf. Inge, *op. cit.*, II, 104–63 (The Absolute), II, 36–103 (Spirit), I, 200–64 (World Soul and derivatives), I, 153–62 (Nature), I, 122–50 (Matter). This paragraph is taken from Windelband and Inge, though I have consulted the works of Plotinus, *ed. cit.* (Quotations from Windelband in this chapter are made by permission of the Macmillan Co., publishers.)

39 Inge, *op. cit.*, II, 198.

40 See Windelband, *op. cit.*, p. 250; Maurice De Wulf, *History of Mediaeval Philosophy*, I, 132, on Proclus: "From this undetermined One comes forth the *nous*, but this emanation is only possible because of intermediate units, which Proclus looks upon as personal gods (Iamblichus). The *nous* divides itself into three spheres, which in their turn are subdivided into triads and hebdomads in such a way that they constitute a framework adapted to pagan Pantheism. Matter is a direct product of one of the triads of the *nous*, and not at all a final emanation of the world-soul as Plotinus held," Note 2. On the development of Neo-Platonism into the mysticism of the Middle Ages, see *ibid.*, I, 83 (Pseudo-Dionysius the Areopagite), 85 (Macrobius), 87 (Boethius), 132 (John Scotus Eriugena), 191 (School of Chartres). On Neo-Platonism as the basis of Cabbalism, see Ginsburg, *op. cit.*, pp. 187–88. For Cabbalists "the demons, constituting the second class of angels, which are the grossest and most deficient of all forms, and are *the shells* of being, inhabit the third habitable or *Assiatic World*. They, too, form ten degrees . . . in which darkness and impurity increase with the descent of each degree," *ibid.*, p. 110.

41 This paragraph is largely a paraphrase of Windelband's beautiful exposition, *op. cit.*, pp. 251–55. Cf. Thomas Aquinas, *Summa Theologica*, I–LXIII, entire.

42 See for example, Anselm, *Dialogus de Casu Diaboli*, Migne, *Patro. Lat.*, 156: 326–60.

43 Windelband, *op. cit.*, pp. 239–40. Cf. Augustine's controversy with the Manichaeans, *Nicene and Post-Nicene Fathers*.

44 Windelband, *op. cit.*, pp. 283–85.

45 *Ibid.*, p. 286. For Plutarch's conception of the origin of evil, which resembles that of the Manichaeans, see Inge, *op. cit.*, I, 90: "The imperfection of the world cannot come from God; for to make God the author of evil is to contradict the idea of God. We must therefore assume two principles, hostile to each other; this hypothesis alone can account for the strife and confusion which we find

everywhere in the world. The evil principle cannot be Matter, for we find evil to be a positive, active thing, such as could not proceed from anything so characterless and indeterminate as Matter. There must be a spiritual power of evil, which may be best designated as an evil World-Soul. From this evil principle proceeds all that is destructive in nature and all that is perverse in man." This conception of an evil World-Soul also reaches the Renaissance.

46 See *The Encyclopaedia Britannica*, 14th ed. s. v. *Predestination;* Windelband, *op. cit.*, pp. 353, 363–66; Philip Schaff, *Saint Augustin, Melanchthon, and Neander* (New York, 1886), pp. 96–106.

47 Thomas Aquinas, *Summa Theologica*, trans. Fathers of the English Dominican Province, I–22–1, 2, 3, 4; I–103–6. I am indebted to the Dominican Fathers not only for translations of direct quotations from St. Thomas but also for felicitous phrasing in my own expositions of the philosopher's thought.

48 *Ibid.*, I–108–5, where he characterizes the orders further.

49 Quoted from Thomas, I–108–6. (Cf. Gregory of Nyssa, *Against Eunomius*, trans. W. Moore and H. A. Wilson, *Nicene and Post-Nicene Fathers*, V, 199; John of Damascus, *Exposition of the Orthodox Faith*, Bk. II, ch. iii, trans. R. S. D. Salmond, *Nicene and Post-Nicene Fathers*, IX, 20.)

50 *Ibid.*

51 Quoted from Thomas, I–108–8, *ad* 2.

52 *Ibid.*, I–110–1.

53 Both quoted from Thomas, *ibid.*

54 Quoted from Thomas, I–64–1, *ob.* 5.

55 *Ibid.*, I–64–1. c.

56 *Ibid.*, I–109–2 (Cf. Cassian, *Conferences*, VIII, *Nicene and Post-Nicene Fathers*, 2nd Ser., XI, 381).

57 *Ibid.*, I–64–4, and I–109–4, *ad* 2.

58 *Against Celsus*, vi, 44, trans. Fr. Crombie, *Ante-Nicene Christian Library*, XXIII, 384.

59 Thomas, I–108–6c; I–109–4, *contra.*

60 References within parentheses in the following paragraphs are to Thomas's *Summa Theologica*.

61 See *supra*, Ch. II.

62 See Rudwin, *op. cit.*, pp. 23–24; Sigmund Feyerabend, *Theatrum diabolorum* (1569); Spalding, *op. cit.*, pp. 43–46.

63 See Scot, *op. cit.*, pp. 420 ff. *passim;* Windelband, *op. cit.*, p. 353; G. W. Osmun, *Augustine: The Thinker* (New York, 1906), pp. 241 ff.

64 Council of Trent, 1563.

65 III, v. In this scene, often considered un-Shakespearean, we have

an illustration of precedence among demons. On this point see Thomas, I–109–AA 1–4, where he quotes Augustine and the Bible; John Cassian, *Conferences*, VIII, *loc. cit.*, p. 381; King James, *op. cit.*, p. 201.

[66] See Aquinas, I–57–3. c.; Augustine, *De divinatione daemonum*, in *Opera omnia, castigata*, etc. Monachorum ordinis Sancti Benedicti, Parisiis, 1837, VI, cap. iii–v; King James, *op. cit.*, p. 45.

[67] Augustine, *op. cit.*, cap. vi; Aquinas, I–114–2, *ad* 2, I–57–4. c.; King James, *op. cit.*, p. 8: "For that olde and craftie Serpent, being a spirite, hee easilie spyes our affections, and so conformes himself thereto, to deceaue vs to our wracke," and p. 21: "to reueale to them the secrets of anie persons, so being they bee once spoken, for the thought none knowes but GOD; except so far as yee may ghesse by their countenance, as one who is doubtleslie learned inough in the Physiognomie."

[68] Cf. Augustine, *De Trinitate*, IV, xi, *loc. cit.*, col. 1255.

[69] *Op. cit.*, p. 39: "For if the deuil may forme what kinde of impressions he pleases in the aire . . . why may he not far easilier thicken & obscure so the air, that is next about them by contracting it strait together, that the beames of any other mans eyes cannot pearce thorow the same, to see them?" Cf. Spalding, *op. cit.*, p. 103.

[70] As most critics are agreed: see Bradley, *op. cit.*, p. 492; Stoll, *op. cit.*, pp. 105, 199, etc.

[71] Cf. Burton, *loc. cit.*, I, 228, where he quotes from Biarmannus in his Oration against Bodine: "He [the devil] begins first with the phantasy, & moves that so strongly that no reason is able to resist. Now he moves the phantasy by mediation of humours; although many Physicians are of the opinion, that the Devil can alter the mind, and produce this disease of himself." Cf. Augustine, *De Trinitate*, IV, xi, *loc. cit.*, col. 1255.

[72] Thomas Nashe, *The Terrors of the Night, or A Discourse of Apparitions* (London, 1594), pp. 223–24; quoted from Campbell, *op. cit.*, p. 91.

[73] Or it may equally well be the voice—illusion or hallucination—of Macbeth's guardian angel departing from him. See Thomas, I–113–6. c.

[74] For the statement of three important positions, see Campbell, *op. cit.*, pp. 84–92, 121.

[75] *Op. cit.*, pp. 199–217.

[76] For a splendid exposition of Catholic faith upon the matter of ghosts, see May Yardley, *The Catholic Position in the Ghost Controversy of the Sixteenth Century*, in Lewes Lavater, *Of Ghostes and Spirites Walking by Nyght*, ed. J. Dover Wilson and May Yardley

(Oxford, 1929), pp. 221–51. Miss Yardley gives an excellent résumé of Pierre Le Loyer's *IIII Livres des Spectres* (1585), written in answer to Lavater's *Of Ghostes.*

[77] On the Protestant position, see Lavater, *op. cit., passim,* but especially Part II; Scot, *A Discourse of Devils and Spirits,* ch. xxvii, *ed. cit.,* pp. 446–47; Yardley, *op. cit.,* pp. 248–50; Iohn Deacon and Iohn Walker, *Dialogicall Discourses of Spirits and Deuils* (1601), pp. 132, 153; King James, *op. cit.,* pp. 59–61; Spalding, *op. cit.,* pp. 44, 53–60.

[78] See Yardley, *op. cit.,* pp. 223–24, 242, 245.

[79] *Ibid.,* pp. 246–48.

[80] John Cassian, *Conferences,* VII, ch. xxiv, *loc. cit.,* XI, 371.

[81] See Furness, p. 473; for a description of Mrs. Siddons' acting of the part, see *ibid.,* p. 303.

[82] *Loc. cit.,* p. 371.

[83] Cassian, *loc. cit.,* p. 366.

[84] Tweedie, quoted from Furness, p. 308.

[85] Thomas Aquinas, I–II–li–9, *ad* 1.

[86] See Pfeil, *Deutsche Revue,* Feb. 1894, p. 239, quoted by Furness, p. 304. The best analysis of the ordinary somnambulistic state is that by W. B. Carpenter, *Mental Physiology* (New York, 1877), pp. 591–601.

[87] T. K. Oesterreich, *Possession Demoniacal and Other, Among Primitive Races, in Antiquity, The Middle Ages, and Modern Times,* trans. D. Ibberson (New York, 1930), p. 39. This is an excellent investigation of the fact of "demonic possession"—however one cares to interpret it; "cases" are presented from many sources. For other cases, see Jean Wier (Johan Wier or Weyer), *Histoires, disputes et discours des illusions et impostures des diables, des magiciens infames, sorcieres et empoisonneurs, des ensorcelez et demoniaques et de la guerison d'iceux* (Paris, 1885); Bodinus, *De magorum Daemonomania* (Hamburg, 1698), etc.

[88] Oesterreich, *op. cit.,* pp. 31–32, 35, 39, *passim.*

[89] Spalding, *op. cit.,* p. 63.

[90] A. H. Tolman, *The Atlantic Monthly,* LXIX, 245.

[91] On the Renaissance attitude toward possession, see Spalding, *op. cit.,* pp. 61–70, and on Shakespeare's use of Harsnet's book, *ibid.,* pp. 70–82; Scot, *op. cit.,* ch. xv, p. 431.

[92] Oesterreich, *op. cit.,* p. 186 ff. Cf. Erich Klingner, *Luther und der deutsche Volksaberglaube, Palaestra,* LVI (1912), 34–38.

[93] *Ibid.,* p. 187. Cf. Deacon and Walker, *op. cit.,* 3rd Dialogue; James, *op. cit.,* p. 72.

[94] *Op. cit.,* pp. 71–73.

[95] Spalding, *op. cit.*, p. 64.

[96] See a spirited review of the controversy in Summers, *op. cit.*, pp. 225–34.

[97] Spalding, *op. cit.*, pp. 61–63.

[98] See the cases in Summers, *op. cit.*, pp. 198–269; Oesterreich, *op. cit.*, *passim;* Burton, *loc. cit.*, I, 227–30, with a bibliography; James, *op. cit.*, p. 72; Felix, Minucius, *The Octavian*, cap. 27, trans. R. E. Wallis, *Ante-Nicene Fathers*, IV, 289–90; Clement, *The Recognitions*, Bk. V, caps. xxxii–xxxiii, trans. Thos. Smith, *Ante-Nicene Fathers*, VIII, 151: "By the friendship of demons, men are brought to disgraceful and base deeds, so that, as is well known, some have laid violent hands upon themselves."

# NOTES TO CHAPTER IV

[1] See Chapters II and III *supra.*

[2] Arthur Symons, *Studies in Elizabethan Drama* (New York, 1919), p. 28.

[3] Salvini, as reported by R. L. Stevenson, quoted in Furness, Variorum *Macbeth*, p. 498.

[4] Sir Henry Irving, quoted by Furness, p. 471.

[5] R. G. Mounton, quoted by Furness, p. 469.

[6] Edward Rose, quoted by Furness, p. 468.

[7] J. C. Bucknill, quoted by Furness, p. 466.

[8] L. L. Schücking, *Character Problems in Shakespeare's Plays* (New York), 1922, p. 77.

[9] J. Q. Adams (ed.), *Macbeth* (Houghton Mifflin), 1931, p. 136.

[10] E. E. Stoll, *Shakespeare Studies* (New York), 1927, pp. 92–3.

[11] Lily B. Campbell, *Shakespeare's Tragic Heroes, Slaves of Passion* (Cambridge), 1930, p. 238.

[12] Benedetto Croce, *Ariosto, Shakespeare, and Corneille* (New York, 1920), p. 225.

[13] A. C. Bradley, *Shakespearean Tragedy* (New York), 1926, p. 352.

[14] G. Wilson Knight, *The Wheel of Fire* (London, 1930), p. 169.

[15] For these general conceptions see Maurice De Wulf, *History of Mediaeval Philosophy*, trans. E. C. Messenger (London, 1926), I, 271–304; De Wulf, *Philosophy and Civilization in the Middle Ages* (Princeton, 1922), pp. 179–219, *passim;* W. Windelband, *A History of Philosophy*, trans. J. H. Tufts (New York), 1931, pp. 318–47.

[16] Windelband, *op. cit.*, p. 191; Eduard Zeller, *Plato and the Older Academy*, trans. Sarah F. Alleyne and A. Goodwin (London, 1888), pp. 419–21.

17 Windelband, *op. cit.*, p. 192. (Quotations from Windelband in this chapter are made by permission of The Macmillan Co., publishers.)

18 *Ibid.*, pp. 282 ff.

19 Philip Schaff, *History of the Christian Church* (New York, 1884), III, 802 ff.

20 Quoted by St. Augustine, *De Gratia Christi, et de Peccato Originali*, I, 18, trans. Peter Holmes and R. E. Wallis, *The Nicene and Post-Nicene Fathers*, 1st Ser., V, 224. In praising Pelagius, however, we must not forget his indebtedness to the "natural religion" of Stoicism and to the "natural" philosophy of the Cappadocian Fathers, Gregory Nazianzen and Gregory of Nyssa.

21 *Op. cit.*, III, 489.

22 The New Schaff-Herzog *Encyclopedia of Religious Knowledge*, ed. S. M. Jackson and G. W. Gilmore, *s. v.* Scholasticism.

23 D. E. Sharp, *Franciscan Philosophy at Oxford*, London, 1930, pp. 203 ff.

24 *Ibid.*, pp. 258–60.

25 *Ibid.*, pp. 336–41; De Wulf, *History* cited, II, 82 ff.; C. R. S. Harris, *Duns Scotus* (Oxford, 1927), II, 289 ff.

26 Harris, *op. cit.*, II, 296 ff.; De Wulf, *History* cited, II, 24 ff.; Martin Grabmann, *Thomas Aquinas, His Personality and Thought*, trans. Virgil Michel (New York), 1928, p. 153.

27 De Wulf, *History* cited, I, 302.

28 See Harris, *op. cit.*, II, 256; Thomas Aquinas, *Summa Theologica*, I–II. 82. 1, 2, 3, 4.

29 Sharp, *op. cit.*, p. 398; R. W. Inge, *The Philosophy of Plotinus* (New York, 1929), II, 186.

30 William of Ockam goes so far as to attribute to the will a power of self-determination that is absolute, regardless of rational motives or the intellectual presentation of the good (De Wulf, *History*, II, 182). His followers—such as Gabriel Biel—well on into the sixteenth century emphasize the "fundamental thesis . . . that man can do anything he will—fulfill the Ten Commandments to the letter or persuade his reason that black is white. The cloister adopted this view and held that by man's own acts, asceticism, prayer, and meditation, he could prepare his soul for union with God" (Preserved Smith, *The Life and Letters of Martin Luther* [New York, 1911], p. 12). It is especially this doctrine of the then "modernists" that seems to arouse the anger of Martin Luther (he calls them "Fools! Theologians for swine!" *Ibid.*, p. 24) and doubtless influences the extreme statement of his own position: "The human will is like a beast of burden. If God mounts it, it wishes and goes as God wills; if Satan mounts it, it wishes and goes as Satan wills. Nor can it

choose the rider it would prefer, nor betake itself to him, but it is the riders who contend for its possession," quoted by Smith, *op. cit.*, p. 208. Surely this Reformation doctrine—stemming from Augustine and perpetuated in the Tenth Article of the Church of England—could have had little effect in developing the Renaissance conception of the essential dignity of the human spirit. At any rate, contemporary nominalism fell before the attacks of the Reformation and Humanism (De Wulf, *History*, II, 290). But Renaissance psychologists and moralists still go back for their inspiration to the great realists, Thomas Aquinas and Duns Scotus. (On the popularity of Scotism and Thomism in the fifteenth and sixteenth centuries, see De Wulf, *History*, II, 210–216, 291–298.) For example, Richard Hooker (*Of the Laws of Ecclesiastical Polity*, I, 7, ed. Isaac Walton [Oxford, 1807], I, 220) is evidently following the Thomist tradition when he says that "the object of Will is that good which Reason doth lead us to seek . . . neither is any other desire termed properly Will, but that where Reason and Understanding, or the show of Reason, prescribeth the thing desired." John Davies of Hereford likewise is of the opinion that the will can desire nothing but what seems to be good (*Microcosmos*, ed. A. B. Grosart, *Complete Works* [Edinburgh, 1873], I, 25). And Giordano Bruno has advanced little beyond the position of Thomas Aquinas, his teacher: "Man's liberty of action is expressed imperfectly, and sometimes in an imperfect object, is continually being disturbed by passion and ignorance of things; for if we acted without any disturbance of the will, or course of thought, without ignorance or passion, then our action would be determined always towards the better of two opposed ends," J. L. McIntyre, *Giordano Bruno* (London, 1903), p. 195. Pierre de la Primaudaye, on the other hand, adheres to the Scotist tradition in likening the will, in its relation to the intellect, to a prince among his council: "And if the consultation be finished, and sentence giuen by iudgment, yet may the Will stay itself from desiring and following after that which is counselled and iudged to be good by reason. So that the whole consultation lieth in the liberty and choice of Will" (*The French Academie; Fully Discoursed and Finished in Foure Bookes* [London, 1618]; cf. *Academie Française*, [Paris, 1580], 12, a, b). And that rationalist, Pierre Charron (*Of Wisdom*, trans. George Stanhope [London, 1697], Bk. I, p. 163) is still more explicit: he acknowledges the collaboration of intellect with will, but the latter finishes "the Action, and determines the whole Matter; and in that respect *Will* is superior even to the *Understanding* it self." Ludovicus Joannes Vives, in spite of his strictures upon scholasticism, has nothing better to offer upon this question than Scotist opinion: "As strength of intelligens is giuen to the mind, to waie euerie thyng, and to know what is good to be done, and what to be lefte vndone: so is the Wil of so greatte power, that ther is nothing in the mind, but it is forced to obey Wyll, if she stand at strife, and wylle yeld no parte of him right to his aduersarie" (*Introduction to Wysedome* [London, 1550], Dv). And Thomas Wright (*The Passions of the Minde in Generall* [London, 1630], first edition in 1601) praises such teachers as Alexander of Hales, Duns Scotus, Ockam, and Richard of Middleton (Preface to the Reader), and bases his theory of the passions upon the scheme of Thomas Aquinas (pp. 22–26, *passim*). For further discussion of Renaissance psychologists, see Ruth Leila Anderson's excellent *Elizabethan Psychology in Shakespeare's Plays* (Iowa City, 1917). For helpful interpretations of the term *individualism* as used in connection with the Renaissance, see Norman Nelson, *Individualism as a Criterion of the Renaissance, JEGPh.*, XXXII (1933), 316–334.

[31] References within parentheses in the following paragraphs are to the *Summa Theologica* of Thomas Aquinas, trans. Fathers of the English Dominican Province. In my expositions from Thomas I frequently use, without further acknowledgment, the very felicitous phrasing of the Dominican Fathers.

[32] Duns, of course, would deny the necessity of end; the presentation of it merely *inclines* the will.

[33] See Chapter III, *supra*.

[34] Compare Bradley's observation on the nature of evil in Shakespeare's tragedies: "Evil exhibits itself everywhere as something negative, barren, weakening, destructive, a principle of death. It isolates, disunites, and tends to annihilate not only its opposite but itself. That which keeps the evil man prosperous makes him succeed, even permits him to exist, is the good in him . . . . When the evil in him masters the good and has its way, it destroys other people through him, but it also destroys him. . . . If existence in an order depends on good, and if the presence of evil is hostile to such an existence, the inner being or soul of this order must be akin to good," *op. cit.*, p. 35. This might have been taken from Thomas Aquinas. (Quoted by permission of The Macmillan Co., publishers.)

[35] On the difference between natural and moral goodness, see De Wulf, *History*, I, 302–03.

[36] See Moulton's adequate explanation of 'the milk of human-kind-ness,' *Shakespeare as a Dramatic Artist* (Oxford, 1893), p. 149. Cf. Furness, p. 71.

37 The contents of this and the following paragraph represent a condensation (as nearly as possible in the author's own clear and exact phraseology) of De Wulf's magnificent "The Scholastic Synthesis," *History* cited, I, 271–304. (By special permission of Longmans, Green and Co., publishers.)

68 See Chapter III, *supra*.

39 Someone may object to my conception of Macbeth's changing character on the grounds that not sufficient time elapses in the course of the drama for such transformations to take place. To such a one it may be pointed out that between Acts II and III a lapse of from one to three weeks is suggested in the text; between Scenes ii and iii of Act IV a long interval must be allowed to account for Ross's journey to Scotland, and between Scene iii of Act IV and Scene i of Act V still another interval covering Malcolm's return to England. See Furness' time analysis, *op. cit.*, p. 504 ff. But, even so, for the psychological and spiritual alterations we are here concerned with, no great lapse of actual time is required; emotional and spiritual life and its growth cannot be measured by the passing of time, but only by the violence and intensity of inner experience. Cf. Alwin Thaler, "The 'Lost Scenes' of *Macbeth*," *PMLA*, XLIX (1934), 843.

40 Demonic forces, symbolized by the Weird Sisters, represent one aspect of Fate in that they, along with other instruments, are designed as executors of the reason of order.

41 See Lily B. Campbell, *op. cit.*, pp. 93 ff.


# NOTES TO CHAPTER V

1 See J. Lewis McIntyre, *Giordano Bruno* (London, 1903), pp. 121 ff.

2 Maurice De Wulf, *History of Mediaeval Philosophy*, trans. E. C. Messenger (New York, 1926), II, 274 ff.; W. Windelband, *A History of Philosophy*, trans. James H. Tufts (New York, 1931), pp. 366 ff. (Quotations from Wildelband in this chapter are made by permission of The Macmillan Co., publishers.)

3 This exposition is based on E. Zeller, *The Stoics, Epicureans, and Sceptics*, trans. O. J. Reichel (London, 1892), pp. 121 ff.; R. M. Wenly, *Stoicism and Its Influence* (Boston, 1924), pp. 74–106.

4 Wenly, *op. cit.*, pp. 114, 123, etc.

5 *Ibid.*, p. 128.

6 *Ibid.*, p. 133.

7 *Ibid.*, p. 134 ff.; Zeller, *op. cit.*, p. 159.

[8] E. K. Rand, *Founders of the Middle Ages* (Cambridge, 1929), pp. 126 ff.; H. M. Ayers, *Rom. Rev.*, X (1919), 1–15, etc.

[9] Cf. E. A. Sonnenschein, "Stoicism in English Literature," *Contemporary Rev.*, CXXIV (1923), 255 ff.; Alois Brandl, *Shakespeare: Leben, Umwelt, Kunst* (Wittenberg, 1923), *passim*.

[10] So says Windelband, *op. cit.*, p. 367.

[11] Charles Bigg, *The Christian Platonists of Alexandria* (Oxford, 1913), pp. 38 ff.

[12] See Windelband, *op. cit.*, pp. 235 ff.

[13] Taken from De Wulf, *History*, I, 115–119. Cf. S. Grandgeorge, *S. Augustin et le neo-Platonism* (Paris, 1896); Ch. Boyer, *Christianisme et Neo-Platonisme dans la formation de S. Augustin* (Paris, 1920).

[14] De Wulf, I, 83–85; Windelband, *op. cit.*, pp. 271, 274.

[15] In his Commentary on the *Somnium Scipionis* of Cicero, I, 14; see De Wulf, I, 85 ff.

[16] For a full outline of his system, see De Wulf, I, 133–139. Cf. Windelband, *op. cit.*, pp. 289 ff.

[17] De Wulf, I, 225–28; Windelband, *op. cit.*, pp. 338 ff., 354 ff.

[18] De Wulf, II, 113–14, 115, 120, 125 ff.

[19] *Ibid.*, II, 245–49; Windelband, *op. cit.*, pp. 345, 368 ff.; McIntyre, *op. cit.*, pp. 143–48.

[20] This exposition is based on McIntyre, *op. cit.*, pp. 127 ff.; De Wulf, II, 259; Symonds, John Addington, *Renaissance in Italy* (New York, 1883), pp. 199–209.

[21] On Ficinus, see De Wulf, *History*, II, 269–271; Symonds, *op. cit.*, pp. 323–329; McIntyre, *op. cit.*, 127 ff.; Windelband, *op. cit.*, pp. 354–358; Lynn Thorndike, *History of Magic and Experimental Science* (New York, 1923), I. ch. XI.

[22] On Patrizzi and his followers, see Windelband, *op. cit.*, pp. 354, 358, 366–77, *passim*.

[23] See Symonds, *op. cit.*, pp. 330–338; and on the works translated, see Christian Ginsburg, *The Kabbalah* (London, 1925), pp. 201, 206.

[24] Quoted from Ginsburg, *op. cit.*, p. 206.

[25] For an excellent exposition of Cabbalism in detail, see Ginsburg, *op. cit.*, pp. 79–127, *passim* cf. S. L. MacGregor Mathers, *The Kabbalah Unveiled* (New York, 1907), Introduction; and three books of *The Zohar*, trans. H. Sperling and M. Simon (London, 1931); A. E. Waite, *The Doctrine and Literature of the Kabbalah* (London, 1902).

[26] See Ginsburg, *op. cit.*, pp. 131–138; *The Sword of Moses*, ed. and trans. M. Gaster, in *Journal of the Royal Asiatic Society* (London, 1896), N. S. XXVIII, 152–55, 158; *The Sixth and Seventh Books of Moses*, 2 vols. (New York, 1889); Mathers, *op. cit.*, pp. 8 ff.

[27] On interpretation of the Cabbala in the light of Christian doctrine, see Ginsburg, *op. cit.*, pp. 138 ff.

[28] See Symonds, *op. cit.*, p. 210.

[29] *De Verbo Mirifico* (Basle, 1494), and *De Arte Cabalistica* (Hagenau, 1516); for a good outline of their contents, see Ginsburg, *op. cit.*, pp. 208–11.

[30] Ginsburg, *op. cit.*, pp. 83, 211–213. Cf. Agrippa, *De occulta philosophia*, lib. III, x ff., xxv ff.; Robert Fludd, *Utriusque Cosmi Maioris scilicet et Minoris Metaphysica, Physica atque Technica Historia*, Oppenhemii, 1617–18; Waite, *op. cit.*, pp. 344 ff.

[31] Quoted from McIntyre, *op. cit.*, pp. 125–26.

[32] See the beautiful synthesis in Windelband, *op. cit.*, pp. 357–8, 366–72, and De Wulf, II, 274–78.

[33] McIntyre, *op. cit.*, p. 125.

[34] *The Utopia of Sir Thomas More*, ed. J. H. Lupton (Oxford, 1895), p. 266; Lupton (note 1) discerns here a reminiscence of Virgil or Statius.

[35] So interpreted by Kurt Schroeder, *Platonismus in der Englischen Renaissance vor und bei Thomas Eliot, nebst neudruck von Eliot's "Disputacion Platonike,"* 1533, in *Palaestra*, LXXXIII (1920), p. 57; on Eliot's conception of God, see p. 109, and *Disputacion*, p. 49.

[36] *The Purple Island*, Cant. I, Stans. 39–44, ed. F. S. Boas, in *The Poetical Works of Giles and Phineas Fletcher* (Cambridge, 1909), II, 20–1.

[37] Such attempts to 'reconcile' the Christian and Neo-Platonic traditions were common enough in this period; see, for example, the 'Christian Universe' of John Colet in Schroeder, *op. cit.*, p. 32.

[38] Quoted from Elias Ashmole's annotations of Thomas Norton's *The Ordinall of Alchimy*, ed. E. J. Holmyard (Baltimore, 1931), p. 116.

[39] See Windelband, *op. cit.*, pp. 373–4; on the processes of multiplying, see Norton, *op. cit.*, pp. 52 ff.; Theofrastus Bombast, of Hohenheim, called Paracelsus the Great, *The Hermetic and Alchemical Writings*, trans. A. E. Waite (London, 1894), I, 19–47, *passim*.

[40] Paracelsus, *op. cit.*, I, 48–71, *passim;* Norton, *op. cit.*, pp. 85 ff.

[41] Paracelsus, *op. cit.*, I, 82–88 (Spirits of the Planets), II, 69–76 (Concerning Elixirs), 94–136 (Concerning the medicinal Philosopher's Stone, Long Life, and Renovation and Restoration), 165 ff. (Alchemy and the Physician), 169 ff. (Prescriptions), 282 ff. (Hermetic Philosophy as related to astrology, magic, necromancy, signatures).

[42] See Giordano Bruno's *De Magia* where natural or "Physical magic is shown to be a natural consequence, first, of the fact that

the same soul, the soul of the world, is in all things, of which the individual finite soul of each thing is a temporary mode or phase; hence all things are linked one with another, through their spiritual identity, in a bond of sympathy; secondly, of the hierarchy of beings—the principle that all finite things are emanations, in increasing degree of imperfection, from the Divine"; quoted from McIntyre, *op. cit.*, p. 116; cf. Ashmole's definition of magic based largely on Agrippa, *op. cit.*, pp. 113–118 (Norton, p. 61).

43 See G. L. Kittredge, *Witchcraft in Old and New England* (Cambridge, 1929); Montague Summers, *The History of Witchcraft and Demonology* (London, 1926), and bibliographies; Lynn Thorndike, *op. cit., passim;* A. E. Waite, *Book of Black Magic, and of Pacts, including the Rites and Mysteries of Goetic Theurgy, Sorcery, and Infernal Necromancy* (London, 1898).

44 See Thorndike, *op. cit.*, II, ch. xlix; Reginald Scot, *The Discoverie of Witchcraft*, ed. Brinsley Nicholson (London, 1886), pp. 392–5 (Theurgy); *Salomonis opus sacrum ab Honorio ordinatum*, Brit. Mus. Sloane MS. 313, and *Tractatus et Experimenta Magica*, Brit. Mus. Sloane MS. 3854, reproduced as, respectively, Nos. 286 and 287 in the MLA Rotographs of Manuscripts and Rare Printed Books, now in the Congressional Library. Sloane MS. 313 belonged to Ben Jonson and is marked at the end 'Theurgia.'

45 Windelband, *op. cit.*, p. 373.

46 See Jacob Burckhardt, *The Civilization of the Renaissance in Italy*, trans. S. G. C. Middlemore (London, 1928), pp. 507 ff.

47 Pater says of Pico's conception of a geocentric universe: "How different from this childish dream is our own conception of nature, with its unlimited space, its innumerable suns, and the earth but a mote in the beam; how different the strange new awe, or superstition, with which it fills our minds," Walter Pater, *The Renaissance* (New York, 1908), p. 43.

48 For an excellent discussion of 'miraculism' in metaphysical poetry, see John Crowe Ransom's "Poetry: A Note in Ontology," *The American Rev.*, III (1934), 192 ff.

49 For a résumé of the discussion, see George Brandes, *William Shakespeare: A Critical Study* (London, 1905), pp. 349–354; Bernhard Munz, *Shakespeare als Philosoph, Anglia*, XLII (1918), pp. 238 ff.

50 See *A Discourse of Devils and Spirits*, attributed to Reginald Scot, ed. Brinsley Nicholson in Scot's *The Discoverie of Witchcraft* (London, 1886), pp. 414–415 (quoting mostly from Psellus and Cardan); Minor White Latham, *The Elizabethan Fairies* (New York, 1930), pp. 46–47; Robert Burton, *The Anatomy of Melancholy*, Part I,

Sect. II, Mem. I, Subs. ii (Bohn, I, 213–219), with an astounding bibliography.

[51] Franz Lutgenau (*Shakespeare als Philosoph*, p. 81 ff.) has already found Shakespeare to be a pantheist in *The Tempest*, see Munz, *op. cit.*, pp. 304–305.

[52] *The Two Books of Francis Bacon on the Proficience and Advancement of Learning, Divine and Human*, appeared no earlier than 1605, and his *Cogitata et Visa* (later called *Novum Organon Scientiarum*, 1620) was not published until 1612. For an excellent statement of the case for modern science in this period, see Richard Foster Jones, *Ancients and Moderns*, Washington University Studies, No. 6, 1936, pp. 1–22.

[53] Pierre Le Loyer, for example, remarks that in Proclus and in Psellus, interpreter of Gregory Nazianzen, the science of theurgy or 'white magic' is divided into three parts: (1) 'Autoptique,' (2) 'Epoptique,' and (3) 'L'Ectheastique.' He faithfully defines these terms, but observes that Iamblichus makes no such distinctions. He reviews a recent controversy between Julius Caesar Scaliger and Cardan on the validity of theurgy, supporting Cardan in opposition to Scaliger, who defends it: *Discours et Histoires des Apparitions des Esprits, Anges, Demons, et Ames, se Monstrans Visibles aux Hommes* (Paris, 1605), Livre VII, Ch. v. pp. 721–726.

# NOTES TO CHAPTER VI

[1] See H. H. Furness, Variorum *The Tempest* (Philadelphia, 1892), pp. 355–388; T. S. Graves, *MLN*, XL (1925), 396–99; E. E. Stoll, *PMLA*, XLVII (1932), 699 ff.; A. Ralli, *A History of Shakespearean Criticism* (London, 1932), *passim;* W. Ebisch and L. L. Schücking, *A Shakespeare Bibliography* (Oxford, 1931), p. 256; E. K. Chambers, *William Shakespeare* (Oxford, 1930), I, 490, etc.

[2] However, see Furness, pp. 306–351; C. M. Gayley, *Shakespeare and the Founders of Liberty in America* (New York, 1917), pp. 225–29; H. D. Gray, *MLN.*, XXXV, 321 ff.; J. D. Rea, *MP.*, XVII, 279–86; R. R. Cawley, *PMLA.*, XLI (1926), 688–726, and references cited in general works above.

[3] Quoted from Furness, Note to I, ii, 296.

[4] *Ibid.*, p. 378. Such views are possibly influenced by the German play, *The Fair Sidea*, where the spirits are the usual mediaeval devils.

[5] N. S. Bushnell, 'Natural Supernaturalism in *The Tempest*,' *PMLA.*, XLVII (1932), 689.

NOTES

⁶ See quotation from Cumont (*Oriental Religions in Roman Paganism*, p. 188) in Lynn Thorndike, *A History of Magic and Experimental Science* (New York, 1923), I, 535, note. The word *theurgy* was first used by Porphyry, says Thorndike, I, 308.

⁷ *The City of God*, X, 9, trans. Marcus Dods (Edinburgh, 1872), I, 394. Cf. Apuleius, *On the God of Socrates, A Discourse on Magic*, and *The Metamorphoses*, trans. in Bohn's *Libraries*.

⁸ Plotinus, *Enneads*, IV, iv, 40, 41, ed. Fr. Creuzer and G. H. Moser in *Opera Omnia* with the commentaries and interpretations of Marsilius Ficinus (London, 1835). See also *Plotinos: Complete Works*, trans. K. S. Guthrie, London; *Plotin Enneads*, ed. and trans. Emile Brehier (Paris, 1924–27); *Select Passages Illustrating Neoplatonism*, ed. and trans. E. R. Dodds (London, 1923–24); R. W. Inge, *The Philosophy of Plotinus* (London, 1929), II, 200–201.

⁹ *Enneads*, II, ix, 14, trans. Dodds, *op. cit.*, p. 115.

¹⁰ St. Augustine, *op. cit.*, I, 394.

¹¹ *The Epistle of Porphyry to the Egyptian Anebo*, trans. Thomas Taylor, in *On the Mysteries of the Egyptians, Chaldeans, and Assyrians* (London, 1895), p. 16; Dodds, *op. cit.*, p. 116.

¹² See Taylor, *On the Mysteries*. This work, which forms the main basis of our discussion, has been doubtfully ascribed to Iamblichus, but for our purposes we may treat it as if it were his. See Taylor, *op. cit.*, Intro.; Thorndike, *op. cit.*, I, 308. The *De sacrificio et magia* of Proclus is a condensation of the *De mysteriis*, see Thorndike, I, 319.

¹³ Quoted from Thomas Whittaker, *The Neoplatonists* (London, 1901), p. 133.

¹⁴ See his discussion of the meaning of *daemon*, *op. cit.*, IX, 19, Dods, I, 376. The Christian Psellos, for example, who did as much as any other man to discredit theurgy, will have it that all daemons are more or less evil; see K. Svoboda, *La Démonologie de Michel Psellos*, Brno, 1927, for his relation to other Neo-Platonists and to the Christian writers. Psellos shows, in his discussion of goety (quoted by Taylor, *op. cit.*, pp. 221–22), that he has failed to reconcile Christian and Neo-Platonic philosophy on the matter of daemons. Julian, however, can still affirm the power of pure theurgy, *Hymn to the Mother of the Gods*, ed. and trans. W. C. Wright (Loeb) (London, 1913), I, 483. I have not had access to the works of Maximus of Ephesus, one of the great theurgists of the fourth century, A. D.

¹⁵ *De Incertitudine et Vanitate scientiarum, declamatio invectiva*, Coloniae, 1527, Parisiis, 1551, apud Agrippinatem, 1531, 1532, 1537, 1539. This passage is quoted from Martino del Rio, *Disquisitionvm*

*Magicarum Libri sex*, Lvgdvni, 1608, 53, 2C, ff.: where a full discussion of the Catholic attitude toward theurgy may be found.

[16] *The Vanity of Arts and Sciences* (London, 1569), 57b (see also the edition of 1684).

[17] *Ibid.*, 59b. Cf.: N. E. D.: *s. v.*, theurgy.

[18] *Discoverie of Witchcraft*, ed. B. Nicholson (London, 1886), Bk. xv, ch. 42, pp. 392–393. Apparently a sort of theurgy was practiced frequently in Scot's time; he subjoins a letter sent to him 'by one which at this present time lieth as a prisoner condemned for this verie matter in the kings bench.'

[19] See the Moser-Creuzer edition cited above.

[20] First reconstructed and published by Gale (Oxford, 1678); see Whittaker, *op. cit.*, p. 136, note 2. I have used Taylor's translation in *On the Mysteries*, pp. 1–16.

[21] The *Liber de mysteriis* was published by Ficinus, Venice, Aldine Press, 1497 and 1516; at Oxford by Gale, 1678. Gale's edition is the basis of Taylor's translation cited above. See Thorndike, I, 307, note. The *de sacrificio et magia* is a Latin translation of what seems to be a fragmentary Commentary of Proclus', made by Ficinus and published at Venice, Aldine Press, 1497, together with the *Liber de mysteriis*. Cf. Thorndike, I, 319, for other editions. I use Taylor's translation, *op. cit.*, pp. 343–347.

[22] He must also have been familiar with Stoic concepts of animistic Nature and universal psychic life in relation to many elements of divination, which were in part transmitted to the Renaissance through the works of Cicero, particularly the *De divinatione*, lib. I, and *De natura deorum*, lib. II. (Cf. Windelband, *op. cit.*, p. 373.) Professor Alois Brandl (*Shakespeare. Leben, Umwelt, Kunst*, Berlin, 1922), who has shown conclusively Shakespeare's direct dependence upon Cicero, says: 'Die Humanisten, voran Erasmus, hatten dem gebildeten England die grösste Achtung und Liebe für den "süssen Tullius" eingeflösst; sie erhoben seine Schriften zur Hauptquelle der antiken Weisheit; vorwiegend aus Cicero schöpfte daher die Elisabethzeit, was sie an Ethik und Naturphilosophie von den Alten zu erfassen vermochte,' p. 309; and again, 'Nichts kann nach der Belesenheit Shakespeares und der Borgweise seiner Zeit dagegen angeführt werden, das er unmittelbar aus Cicero geschöpft habe; doch gab es auch eine Menge buchmässiger Zwischenglieder, die den Faden von der Tiber zur Themse spinnen könnten, lateinische wie Senecas Essays, englische wie Elyot, französische wie Montaigne; nicht zu vergessen der lebenden Humanisten, die zahlreich in Shakespeares Umgebung vorhanden waren und in mündlichem Gespräche nachhelfen könnten,' p. 328; see in addition pp. 106–43, *passim*, 18 ff., 75, 202, etc., for

noteworthy illustrations of Shakespeare's borrowing. The dramatist may also have been acquainted with the so-called Notory Art (cf. Thorndike, II, 279 ff.; Ben Jonson's MS. copy of *Salomonis opus sacrum ab Honorio ordinatum, tractatus de arte magica*—designated *Theurgia* on the fly-leaves—Sloane 313, British Museum; *The Sword of Moses*, ed., and trans. M. Gaster [London, 1896]), which seeks communion with divinity through invocations to angels and demons, and through the uttering of mystic names.

[23] This exposition is based largely upon W. Windelband's *A History of Philosophy*, trans. J. H. Tufts (New York, 1931), pp. 244; 251. Cf. Inge, *op. cit., passim.* (Quotations from Windelband in this chapter are made by permission of The Macmillan Co., publishers.)

[24] See De Wulf, *A History of Mediaeval Philosophy*, trans. E. C. Messenger (New York, 1926), I, 132, Note 2, on Proclus.

[25] The references within parentheses in the following paragraphs are to Taylor's *On the Mysteries*. I sometimes use Taylor's phraseology without further acknowledgment. (By permission of Mr. P. J. Dobell, son of the distinguished publisher.)

[26] See Proclus, *On Providence, Fate and Free-Will*, trans. K. S. Guthrie, in *Proclus's Life, Hymns & Works* (The Platonist Press, Yonkers, N. Y., 1925), pp. 1–9; Proclus, *De sacrificio et magia*, trans. Taylor, *op. cit.*, pp. 343–347, and cf. pp. 240–242.

[27] Proclus, *On Providence*, p. 8.

[28] *Ibid.*, pp. 9–10. There are, of course, other classical and mediaeval conceptions of Fate. See, for example, Ficinus' commentary on Plotinus' *Enneads*, III, i, *ed. cit.*, I, 399. Cf. H. R. Patch's excellent study, "Necessity in Boethius and the Neoplatonists," *Speculum*, X (1935), 393–404.

[29] *Consolation of Philosophy*, Bk. IV, Pr. vi. Cf. Thomas Aquinas, *Summa Theologica*, I–CXVI. For a philosophically uncritical study of Fate or Destiny, see H. R. Patch, 'Troilus on Determinism,' *Speculum*, VI (1931), 225–243; cf. W. C. Curry, 'Destiny in Chaucer's *Troilus*,' *PMLA*, XLV (1930), 129–168.

[30] Quoted from Taylor, *op. cit.*, p. 339. For similar classifications in Proclus, Iamblichus, and others, see Svoboda, *op. cit.*, p. 15 ff.; *A Discourse of Devils and Spirits*, ed. B. Nicholson in Reginald Scot's *Discoverie of Witchcraft*, pp. 414–415. Cf. Robert Burton, *The Anatomy of Melancholy*, Part I, Sect. II, Mem. i, Subs. ii.

[31] So Proclus, see Taylor, *op. cit.*, p. 204; Iamblichus, V, 14, 17, and IV, 1, 2. For a résumé of Neo-Platonic opinion on daemons, see Ficinus' commentary on the works of Plotinus, *loc. cit., passim*, but especially pp. 79, 220, 524.

[32] So Proclus, see Svoboda, *op. cit.*, p. 18.

[33] *Enneads*, III, v, 6. (Cf. Iamblichus, II, 5.)

[34] *Ibid.*, IV, iv, 43.

[35] See Svoboda, *op. cit.*, pp. 24–25 for a survey of the writers who have held like opinions.

[36] See Svoboda, p. 25. Psellus concludes that daemons are composed of air or fire or of both, that they are generally invisible, in form round or oblong, sensible, capable of taking nourishment and of reproducing their kind, and destructible; see Svoboda, p. 19.

[37] Proclus (*In Tim.*, 142 D) quotes Porphyry to this effect; Psellus agrees, Svoboda, p. 28.

[38] See Svoboda, pp. 20–24, for a review of Neo-Platonic and Christian opinion on the question of changing forms of daemons.

[39] *Enneads*, IV, iv, 35.

[40] *Ibid.*, IV, iv, 40.

[41] Quoted from Taylor, p. 222.

[42] I quote from Dodds' translation, *op. cit.*, p. 117.

[43] See Proclus, in Taylor, *op. cit.*, p. 344 ff.

[44] *Ibid.*, pp. 342–347.

[45] The 'auspicious star' which Prospero courts (I, ii, 182) would be identified by Neo-Platonists with one of the gods. The heavenly spheres are 'celestial animals of the Gods' (I, 17), and in a certain anagogic sense 'the visible celestials are all of them Gods, and after a certain manner, incorporeal' (I, 17). Prospero's intellectual soul has been elevated to the point where he can look upon one of the gods, therefore, and he finds that its effluxions are beneficent.

[46] The reader might be interested in a curious anthology of magic formulae, conjurations, mystic names of God and angels, seals and magic circles, called *The Sixth and Seventh Books of Moses* (New York, 1889), which purports to be a translation of extracts from various Cabbalistic works and writings on the Notory Art. I recommend for consideration the extract (II, 36 ff.) said to be taken from a magical work published in Rome, 1501, under the patronage of Pope Alexander VI. Here the practitioner is directed to trust solely in the might and power of God, to cite spirits at certain hours of the night, and to make all conjurations from within a magic circle written with the blood of young white doves (see Figure 24).

Upon entrance to this circle, the magician must utter these powerful names: "Tetragrammaton, Theos, Ischiros, Athanatos, Messias, Imas, Kyrie Eleison, Amen," and consecrate the operation with a quotation from the ninety-first Psalm. Then follow citations of the Seven Great Princes, one of whom is Ariel, "a very serviceable spirit, and appears in the form of a ferocious dog. He commands the lost treasures of land and sea." To call up Ariel, one must describe his seal or character (see Figure 25 ver.) "upon virgin parchment, with the blood of butterflies, at the time of full moon," and utter the following mystic names: "Ischyros, Theor Zebaoth, Wyzeth, Xyzo, Xywethorowoy, Xanthos, Wiros, Rurawey, Ymowe, Moswathosway, Wuvnethowesy, Zebaoth. Yvme, Zvswethohowe. Yschrioskay, Ulathos, Wysoy, Yrsswo, Xyzeth, Durpbijthaos, Wuzowethus, Yzweoy, Zaday, Zywaye, Hagethorwos, Yschyros, Imas, Tetragrammaton, Ariel." And if Ariel does not appear in answer to this citation, the practitioner may employ the following conjuration provided by Moses, Aaron, and Solomon: "Zijmuorsobet, Noijm Zavaxo, Quehaij, Abawo. Noquetonaij. Oasaij, Wuram, Thefotoson, Zijoronaifwetho. Mugelthor, Yzxe. Agiopuaij, Huzije, Suthatijm, Sowe Oxursoij. Zijbo, Yzweth, Wuaij. Salarthon, Quaij, Quehaij Quijrou, Sardowe, Xoro, Wugofhoswerhij, Kaweko, Ykquos, Zehatho. Aba. Amen." This citation is irresistible when accompanied with the casting of frankincense and myrrh upon burning coals. I give these extracts for what they are worth. Though Shakespeare may have derived the name *Ariel* from some such work as this, the magic here involved is not purely that which Prospero employs.

[47] Robert Kirk, *Secret Commonwealth*, p. 5; quoted from Minor White Latham, *The Elizabethan Fairies* (New York, 1930), p. 46.

[48] *Loc. cit.*, p. 495; cf. Latham, *op. cit.*, p. 41.

[49] *Ibid.*, p. 510; cf. Latham, p. 59, etc.

[50] Furness says regarding demi-puppets: 'There must have been some reason for the use of "demy," but what it is I cannot say. To translate it as Schmidt does, and define it as "half-a-puppet," is merely what Dr. Johnson would call "motion without progress." ' *Op. cit.*, p. 235.

[51] I cannot understand, therefore, why Furness should say, 'This wavering of thought at the crisis of his fate is pathetic,' Note to V, i, 57.

[52] Dodds, *op. cit.*, p. 115, note 3.

[53] *Enneads*, IV, iv, 41, trans. Dodds, p. 114.

[54] *Ibid.*, V, i, 6; trans. Dodds, p. 115, note 3.

[55] I recommend strongly, for example, H. D. Gray's illuminating study of parallels between certain magic incidents in *The Tempest* and passages in the *commedia dell' arte* scenarios appearing in a manuscript of Locatelli, 1622, *MLN*, XXX, 321 ff.

[56] See chapters II, III, and IV, *supra*.

[57] However, Shakespeare's great passage on the evanescence of the world and what is in it (IV, i, 148–58) is distinctly Christian and

conventional in spirit. Cf. Windelband, *op. cit.*, pp. 251–55, on the Christian conception of the world as beginning and passing away in time.

[58] This chapter appeared first in Herrig's *Archiv für das Studium der Neueren Sprachen*, CLXVIII (1935), 25–36, 185–196.

# NOTES TO APPENDIX A

[1] Benedetto Croce, *Aesthetic as Science of Expression and General Linguistic*, trans. Douglas Ainslee (New York), 1922; Theodor Lipps, *Ästhetik: Psychologie des Schönen und der Kunst* (Leipzig, 1920); H. C. Sanborn, *A Personalistic View of Art*, in *Studies in Philosophy*, ed. E. C. Wilm (New York, 1922).

[2] Croce, pp. 15–16.

[3] *Ibid.*, p. 35.

[4] *Ibid.*, p. 89.

[5] Gustav Freytag, in *European Theories of the Drama*, ed. Barrett H. Clark (Cincinnati, 1918), pp. 368–9.

[6] *Op. cit.*, p. 20.

# INDEX